The Gourmet's Vegetarian Cookbook

Myra Street

Regency House Publishing Ltd.

Published in 1997 by
Regency House Publishing Limited
3 Mill Lane
Broxbourne
Hertfordshire, EN10 7AZ

ISBN 1 85361 456 4

Printed in China

All photographs in this book are supplied by permission of Food Features.
Illustrations by Tony Truscott.

Contents

Introduction

Government departments and nutritionists are constantly urging us to adapt our diet to include as many unrefined foods as possible, high in fiber and low in sugar and saturated fats. The message appears to have got through and vegetarian food is the success story of the past decade. This emphasis on meals containing cereals and pulses, and very much more fruit and vegetables, can do nothing but good and dishes without meat are increasing in popularity as more and more people become health- and weight-conscious.

Following a vegetarian diet has never been easier as the vast array of vegetables and exciting ingredients in stores and supermarkets readily confirms. Commercially chilled and frozen ready meals are now freely available but it is often just as quick and easy to prepare interesting meatless dishes for yourself, as this book aims to show.

There are varying degrees of vegetarianism. Vegans eliminate all foods of animal origin, such as gelatin and even honey from their diet as well as meat, fish and dairy produce, and take their protein primarily in the form of nuts and pulses. Lacto vegetarians totally avoid meat or fish but do eat eggs and dairy foods. Others eschew meat but include fish in their diet and a growing number of people, while not regarding themselves as totally committed vegetarians, are eating less and less meat and including more and more 'vegetarian' foods in a search for improved health and increased vitality which will hopefully lead to a longer active life.

It is the aim of this book to suggest ways of adding variety to the diets of all these groups. However, there are pitfalls attached to any new régime. Many people think that if they cut out meat their diet will be automatically healthier. It is just as important for vegetarians to maintain a healthy balance in order that the body can grow, repair itself and remain in good working order. Teenagers, who may be still growing, may decide to give up meat without realizing that they must look to other sources of protein.

A vegetarian needs a good combination of starchy foods (bread, pasta, rice), proteins (nuts and pulses) and dairy products (milk and yogurt), as well as an abundance of fresh fruits and vegetables. It is all too easy to replace the saturated fats found in meat with the the similar types of fats contained in dairy products, such as hard cheeses. In this respect, the many low fat products commercially available have a useful part to play.

The range of products is vast and this book specifies the use of cheese, milk, butter and margarine as well as the various vegetable oils. Depending on the degree and type of vegetarian diet you favor, you can make substitutions as you wish. You can use olive oil or vegan margarine, full fat or low fat cheeses, including those made without animal rennet. It is all a question of balancing your requirements and making sure you are getting your full quota of daily nutriments.

Vegetarians need all the essential nutrients as follows:

Protein: Essential for the growth and repair of body cells, the main sources being cheese and milk products, eggs, nuts, seeds, whole grains, and pulses including soya and TVP products.

Carbohydrate: Helps produce energy and warmth and can be obtained from products made from flour (such as bread and pasta), rice, cereals, beans, peas and lentils, sugar (which produces calories but no nutriment), honey, fruit, and vegetables.

Fats: The unsaturated types derived from plants are an essential part of the strict vegetarian diet as well as providing warmth and energy. They also help the absorption of vitamins A, D, E and K.

Some vegetarians also take saturated fats in the form of dairy produce, such as butter, cream, cheese and milk, as well as eggs.

Vitamins and Minerals: Necessary for body building and maintenance, the functioning of essential organs and an efficient metabolism as well as helping the body to resist infection. They are found in practically all foods but long storage and cooking can destroy them. It is therefore important to eat as much raw or lightly cooked fresh vegetables and fruit in order to ensure a good supply.

Fiber: Many Western diets contain insufficient fiber which, although not a nutrient (it passes straight through the system), is essential for the efficient functioning of the digestive system. It is found in nuts, beans, lentils, bread (especially wholewheat), dried fruit, cereals, pasta (especially wholewheat), brown rice, bran and bran products. Fruit and vegetables contain varying amounts but are not as high in fiber as many would suppose. Fiber should therefore be taken from a variety of sources. Because the vegetarian diet would typically contain many of these foods, it follows that it is naturally high in fiber.

Vegetables

Artichokes (Globe) To clean, place head down in a bowl of salted water for 1 hour. Remove and cook in a large pan of salted water, acidulated with 2 tablespoons lemon juice to $1^3/_4$ pints (1 litre) of water. Bring to the boil and cook for 25-30 minutes depending on size. To test, pull out a large leaf and if it comes away easily and the flesh is tender at the base, the artichoke is cooked. Drain upside down before serving. The hairy choke should be removed before serving to reveal the heart. An excellent snack or first course served hot with Hollandaise sauce or cold with a vinaigrette dressing or mayonnaise.

Artichokes (Jerusalem) These are knobbly tubers which can grow quite large. They are difficult to peel and it is often better to parboil them in salted water for 10 minutes before attempting to remove the skin. After this, cook as for the individual recipe. To prevent discoloration after peeling, immerse in water to which lemon juice or vinegar has been added. These make excellent soups and vegetable dishes but do no eat too many at one time as they are one of the more flatulence-producing vegetables.

Asparagus Cut off about 2 inches of the thick woody part at the base and peel the remainder of the stem with a potato peeler. Form the stems into a bundle and stand them upright (tied with string) in a tall pan of boiling salted water and covered with a dome of aluminum foil. Bring back to the boil and, depending on the thickness of the asparagus, cook from 15-40 minutes. You can cook asparagus satisfactorily in the microwave oven – 6-8 minutes for thin spears and 8-10 minutes for thicker ones. To 8oz (225g) asparagus, add 2 tablespoons water in a china dish.

Aubergines (Eggplants) Choose shiny bright-skinned eggplants (discard wrinklies). Unless they are to be stuffed in their skins, you may like to peel them but many people prefer to leave the skins on. Eggplants are usually sprinkled with salt and allowed to stand for at least 30 minutes before cooking to allow them to give up their bitter juices. This also helps them absorb less oil when frying. Rinse and pat dry with kitchen paper before using. If they are to be included in casserole dishes, lasagna and ratatouille, cook in the microwave – 1lb (450g) of sliced eggplants in 2 tablespoons water will take 8 minutes. This is healthier than a preliminary frying.

Avocados Hard avocados are not a pleasure to eat, so keep them in a warm kitchen for 2-3 days if you are shopping ahead. To serve as a starter, cut the avocado in half and remove the pit. Paint over immediately with lemon juice to prevent discoloration. Serve with a vinaigrette dressing or mayonnaise. Avocados make excellent salads combined with citrus fruits, such as grapefruit and oranges, and dips to serve with crudités and potato chips.

Broad Beans (Fava Beans) The beans are removed from the pod, best when young (wear rubber gloves to avoid the hands from becoming black), and cooked in a little boiling salted water for about 10 minutes until tender. Alternatively, you could use good quality frozen beans. Both are delicious served with a parsley or butter sauce.

Green Beans The tiny French *haricots verts* can be topped and tailed and cooked whole in a little boiling salted water for 5 minutes or until tender. Alternatively, you can cook 1lb (450g) in a microwave in 2 tablespoons water for 6-8 minutes.

String Beans Remove the strings and slice before cooking in a little boiling salted water for 8-10 minutes. Cook in a microwave as for French beans.

Bean Sprouts These are useful in salads and stir-fries. Though readily available in supermarkets and oriental stores they are nevertheless very easy to grow at home, even without a garden.

Broccoli Trim the stalks and cut into spears. Cook in boiling salted water for 8-10 minutes. 1lb (450g) will cook in a microwave in 2 tablespoons of water in 10-12 minutes.

Cabbage Wash carefully and shred or tear before cooking. Shred finely for coleslaws and salads (red or white cabbage is excellent mixed with nuts and raisins). Cook in a small amount of boiling salted water for 5-8 minutes or cook 1lb (450g) in 2 tablespoons water in the microwave for 8-10 minutes.

Cauliflower Wash and break into florets or wash and leave whole with the outside leaves, cutting a cross into the stalk. Cook in 2inches (5cm) boiling salted water or steam in a basket until tender, about 10-15 minutes depending on size. 1lb (450g) florets will take 10-12 minutes in 2 tablespoons water in the microwave.

Celery Wash and remove the coarse strings from the stalks before slicing for cooking or serving raw in salads.

Courgettes (Zucchini) Wash, top and tail and cut into slices or halves for stuffing. They can be fried, casseroled, braised or stuffed. 1lb (450g) will cook in 8-10 minutes in 2 tablespoons water in the microwave.

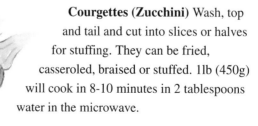

Leeks These versatile vegetables have many uses in soups, gratins, vegetable casseroles and are good served with a sauce. Trim away the rough green parts and cut a cross through from the green part to the thick white part of the stem. Rinse thoroughly under the cold tap to remove any dirt and mud. Shake, dry and cut up or leave whole as the individual recipe dictates. Sliced leeks will take about 6 minutes to fry in butter or oil. 1lb (450g) in 2 tablespoons water will take 7-8 minutes to cook in the microwave.

Peppers These include the sweet red, green and yellow peppers as well as the fiery chili peppers used to add heat. They should be glossy, shiny and wrinkle-free. Peppers have a high vitamin C content and are always deseeded before use. In many recipes they are blanched or lightly cooked if they are to be served raw. This is a matter of choice but they can be indigestible when used completely raw in salads. Wash hands thoroughly after deseeding chili peppers and refrain from touching the eyes. Many cooks prefer to use rubber gloves.

Spinach Thoroughly wash the leaves, removing the thick stalks, then cook for a few minutes in the water clinging to the leaves together with an additional 1-2 tablespoons water. Drain and press all the water out with the back of a wooden spoon. Pre-washed young spinach in bags is available which can be cooked as it is in the microwave or used in salads. This is a more expensive option but very quick to prepare. Cook 1lb (450g) washed spinach in the microwave with no additional water for about 5 minutes.

Tomatoes To skin tomatoes, plunge them into boiling water for 30 seconds, remove with a fork, and peel back the skin which will be easy to remove. A single tomato can be briefly held over the naked flame of a cooking stove before skinning. However, this is not practical for larger quantities.

Onions, Garlic and Shallots These are all bulbs of the lily family which have to be peeled before using.

Root Vegetables It is advisable to peel carrots, turnips, swedes and parsnips before cooking because of the various pesticides used in their cultivation. Use a potato peeler to remove as thin a layer of skin as possible as this is where most of the nutriments are stored. They can then be diced, sliced or left whole according to the recipe. Raw carrots can be grated for salads or cut into sticks as part of a raw vegetable platter.

Potatoes (New) There are many types of potatoes freely available in stores and supermarkets. Many retailers clearly mark them with the name of the variety and even suggest types of dishes for which they are suitable, for example, French fries or potato salad. New potatoes are better boiled in their skins which can be removed after cooking if really necessary.

(Old) Wash and scrub and preferably boil or bake, removing the skins after cooking. A potato ricer is a handy tool for producing perfect mashed potatoes – smooth, velvety and free from lumps.

Dried Pulses or Legumes

All dried beans and peas should be soaked for at least 8 hours or overnight before cooking. The soaking water should be discarded and the beans covered with fresh water, brought to the boil and simmered until cooked al dente, rather like pasta. Do not add salt to the water when cooking pulses, otherwise they will not soften. Season after cooking. Once cooked they can then be used in various ways. Digestive problems can be alleviated by adding $^1/_2$ teaspoon caraway seeds, aniseed, fennel or asafoetida to the cooking water of every 8oz (225g) beans. Many varieties come ready prepared in cans thus eliminating the long soaking and cooking process.

Adzuki Beans Small red beans with a strong nutty flavor. They are excellent for stuffings, pies, veggie burgers and nut loaves. Soak, bring to the boil, then simmer for 45 minutes until tender.

Black-eyed Beans or Cow Peas These have an earthy flavor and are suitable for soups, rissoles and casseroles. Do not soak but bring to the boil, then simmer for 40 minutes.

Flageolet Beans Suitable for salads, pâtés and purées. Soak, bring to the boil, then simmer for 1 hour.

Haricot or Navy Beans The 'baked bean' bean, these are excellent in soups and stews. Soak, bring to the boil, then simmer for 1 hour.

Kidney Beans These are best in hot, spicy dishes such as chilis and casseroles. After soaking the beans must be boiled rapidly for 10 minutes to destroy harmful enzymes before simmering for 1-1$^1/_4$ hours.

Chick Peas Nutty in flavor and a pale golden color, they make excellent dips and pâtés as well as useful bases for salads. Soak, bring to the boil then simmer for 1-1$^1/_2$ hours.

Split Peas These are yellow or green and when cooked produce good dals and purées. Wash and cook for 15 minutes.

Lentils Green or brown, they are good in soups and casseroles as they do not disintegrate in cooking. No soaking is necessary: cook for 45 minutes.

Cheese

Most hard cheeses are set with rennet which is an enzyme derived from a calf's stomach. They are therefore unsuitable for strict vegetarians. However, many cheeses are now being made with non-animal rennet and are marked 'vegetarian cheese'. Cottage, curd, feta and goat's cheeses are made without rennet and can be used freely and where suitable.

Fromage frais, which originated in France, is made from pasteurized skimmed milk with some cream added and contains varying amounts of fat. Use the low fat type in preference to the others.

Meat Substitutes

Tofu This is a soya bean curd which has a high protein content and is a suitable nutritional substitute for meat, fish and poultry. The benefit of tofu is that it is low in fat as well as being high in protein. It is rich in iron, calcium and B vitamins.

Smoked tofu is firm and has been smoked over wood for 3-6 hours. Marinate it with other vegetable for kebabs, or use it fried and in casseroles. Silken tofu is suitable for making creamy dressings for salad and for dips. Braised tofu is also available in cans.

Tempeh This is made from soya beans fermented in banana leaves and is sold frozen in what looks rather like bacon slices. It smells like mushrooms and tastes a little like chicken. It is also sold in squares which can be cut into wedges and fried. Serve with rice and other vegetables.

TVP (Textured Vegetable Protein) These meat substitutes are an excellent source of protein and can be added to vegetable dishes to make them more filling. They can be purchased in granules, rather like ground meat, or in cubes. There are vegetarian sausages, burgers and made-up dishes. All these can be purchased in many supermarkets as well as health food stores.

Oils and Fats

Use vegetable oils, such as safflower, sesame, corn and sunflower which are high in polyunsaturates and are said to lower the cholesterol content of the blood. Olive oil is best for taste and is excellent for salads. Animal fats such as butter, hard cheese and cream are high in saturated fats and should be eaten in moderation.

Agar (Agar-agar)

A setting agent made from seaweed and a vegetarian substitute for gelatin. Use 2 teaspoons to 2 cups liquid or according to pack instructions.

Soups

Fresh vegetable soups are easy to prepare, nourishing, and low in calories if eaten with wholegrain bread and without added fat in the form of butter or margarine. They are an excellent way of adding variety to a vegetarian diet and can often be a substantial meal in their own right.

Broths

The more simple broths are produced from root vegetables cooked in stock or water with seasoning. Pulses, legumes and barley can be added for extra protein and pasta and dumplings for extra energy. Prepare potatoes, onions, carrots, swedes, celery, turnips, parsnips and leeks as directed on pages 9-10. For soup, the vegetables should be cut into even-sized pieces, the size depending on individual taste. If the vegetables are cut into thick chunks they will take longer to cook.

Puréed Soups

This is simply a method of making thick soups by pulverizing the vegetables in a blender, food processor or food mill. If a very smooth soup is required, then it can be passed through a sieve. These soups rarely require thickening as the puréed vegetables provide enough texture of their own. Cream or milk can be added to make a cream soup and a whirl of cream looks attractive floating on the surface of the finished dish. 1 tablespoon cornstarch to 1 quart liquid can be used to thicken any type of soup if it requires it. Alternatively, a potato cooked in with the soup will thicken it naturally.

Storing Soups

Vegetable soups freeze well, therefore it is time-saving to make double quantities and freeze a portion for future use. Take care to keep vegetable stocks and soups in the refrigerator where they will keep well for several days. Root vegetables have a tendency to sour, so it is better to use soups containing them within three days and freeze any left-overs.

Vegetable Stock or Bouillon

Wherever possible, use the water in which vegetables have been cooked or home-made vegetable stock for preparing vegetarian dishes. Also available are commercially-produced vegetable bouillon cubes and stock powders suitable for vegetarians which can be used as a stand-by. One cube or a teaspoon of powder can be added to vegetable stock for extra flavor.

Vegetable Stock

Use as a light stock for pale soups

Makes 2 quarts
2 tablespoons olive oil
4 potatoes, peeled and cut into slices
1 large onion, chopped
2-3 carrots, sliced
2-3 stalks celery, sliced
1 small piece of turnip, cubed
1 bouquet garni
A little parsley and thyme
1-2 bay leaves
8 cups water

- Heat the oil in a large saucepan, add the prepared vegetables and stir around in the oil. Cook for 5 minutes over a low heat without allowing the vegetables to color.
- Pour in the water and allow the vegetables to simmer for about 1 hour. Add a little more water from time to time.
- Strain the stock and cool. Store in the refrigerator for up to 3 days or, if longer storage is required, put into the freezer.

Preparation Time: 10 minutes.
Cooking Time: 1 hour 10 minutes.

Variation
Dark Vegetable Stock
Use another tablespoon of oil and fry the vegetables briskly until brown. Add some miso or soy sauce to give a darker color. Add vegetable cooking water to stock for extra flavor.

Minestrone

Serves 4
1/4 cup dried navy beans
2 tablespoons oil
1/4 cup butter
1 onion, diced
1 garlic clove, crushed
2 carrots, cut in rings
2 stalks celery, chopped
2 medium-sized potatoes
1 zucchini, diced
3 cups canned plum tomatoes

1 sprig rosemary
1 tablespoon tomato paste
2 quarts vegetable stock
2 leeks, finely chopped
Salt and pepper
$\frac{1}{4}$ cup small pasta shapes
For the garnish
2 tablespoons Parmesan cheese
1 tablespoon chopped parsley

- Soak the beans for at least 8 hours in cold water, then bring to the boil in fresh water and cook for about 45 minutes to 1 hour.
- Heat the oil and butter in a large saucepan and add the onion and garlic over a low heat. After 3 minutes, add the carrots and celery and stir gently for about 2 minutes.
- Add the potato, zucchini and tomatoes, then stir in the stock and tomato paste. Season well before adding the beans and simmer for about 20 minutes.
- Add the leeks and continue simmering for a further 10 minutes. Throw in the pasta and continue cooking until it is tender but firm. Serve with grated Parmesan cheese and parsley or Pesto Sauce (page 81).

Preparation Time: 15 minutes plus 8 hours soaking for the beans.
Cooking Time: 40 minutes.

Variation
$\frac{1}{4}$ green cabbage, finely shredded, can be added with the leeks and a few fresh or frozen peas toward the end, cooked for 5 minutes.

If using canned beans, do not add until 10 minutes before the end of the cooking time.

ABOVE RIGHT: *Vegetable Stock with pasta and herbs*
RIGHT: *Minestrone*

Beet Soup

Serves 4

*1 pound uncooked beets, peeled and cut
into strips
1 carrot, cut into thin rings
6 scallions, chopped
1 medium potato, sliced
1 quart vegetable stock (page 12)
Juice of 1 lemon
Salt and pepper*
For the garnish
*$^1/_2$ cup sour cream
1 tablespoon chopped chives (optional)*

- Put the beets, carrot and green onions in the stock and simmer until the vegetables are tender, about 35 minutes.
- Sieve or pass through a blender or food processor. Season to taste with lemon juice and salt and pepper. Add beetroot stock, if available, to enhance the color.

Beet Soup

- Garnish with swirls of cream and chives.
Preparation Time: 15 minutes.
Cooking Time: 35 minutes.

Variation

Borscht

Add 1 carrot and 2 medium potatoes cut into matchsticks along with the beets and other vegetables (as above). 1 onion, diced, 2 stalks celery, sliced, 2 zucchini, diced, and a bouquet garni should be added with 1 large ripe tomato, skinned and chopped. Simmer until vegetables are cooked. Remove bouquet garni before serving topped with sour cream.

Beet Stock

This adds extra color to beet soup, providing the soup is not boiled.

Wash 1 pound uncooked beets, removing all earth from the skin. Grate into a saucepan with 2 cups vegetable stock and 3 tablespoons wine vinegar. Bring to the boil and simmer gently for about 30 minutes. Allow to stand and cool for at least 1 hour. Strain into a jug and use as required.

Celery & Stilton Soup

Serves 4

*$^1/_4$ cup butter
2 medium onions, finely chopped
1 large head of celery, finely sliced
2 tablespoons all-purpose flour
1 quart vegetable stock (page 12)
Pepper, 1 bouquet garni
Sprig of parsley, $^1/_4$ cup blue cheese*
For the garnish
*Celery leaves
2 tablespoons blue cheese, diced
or crumbled*

- Heat the butter in a large saucepan, add the onions and cook over a low heat for 4 minutes, stirring from time to time. Add the celery and continue stirring in the butter for a further 3 minutes.
- Sprinkle over the flour and stir well until it is all absorbed by the vegetables.
- Gradually add the stock, pepper and

bouquet garni, stir well before covering with a lid and simmering for 35 minutes or until the celery is tender.

- Remove and discard the bouquet garni and parsley.
- The soup can be blended or processed at this stage or the vegetables left in chunky pieces if preferred.
- Mash the cheese in a bowl and add to the soup just before serving. Do not boil the soup after the cheese has been added. Serve in heated bowls garnished with a little crumbled cheese and a few celery leaves.

Preparation Time: 10 minutes.
Cooking Time: 45 minutes.

Tomato & Vegetable Soup

Serves 4
3 tablespoons vegetable oil
2 medium onions, finely diced
2 carrots, cut into small dice
3 stalks celery, finely chopped
1 piece of turnip, cut into small dice
1 sprig of thyme, 1 bouquet garni
1 bay leaf
1 quart vegetable stock (page 12)
1 leek, finely diced
2 cartons crushed tomatoes
2 tablespoons tomato paste
1 teaspoon sugar, salt and pepper
For the garnish
Thyme or parsley sprigs
4 tablespoon light cream (optional)

- Heat the oil in a large saucepan, add the onion and carrot and stir well for about 2 minutes over a medium heat.
- Add the celery and turnip and continue stirring for a further 2 minutes. Add the herbs and the stock, bring to the boil and simmer for 20 minutes.
- Add the leek, tomatoes, tomato paste, sugar and seasoning, stir well and allow to simmer for a further 20 minutes or until the vegetables are tender.
- Serve garnished with the fresh herbs. Cream can be served separately or drizzled on top.

Preparation Time: 10 minutes.
Cooking Time: 45 minutes.

Lentil Soup

Serves 4
2 tablespoons vegetable oil
2 medium onions, finely chopped
1 potato, thinly sliced
2 stalks celery, finely chopped
2 medium carrots, grated
$^3/_4$ cup red lentils, washed and drained
6 cups vegetable stock (page 12)
1 bay leaf, 1 bouquet garni
Salt and pepper
4 tablespoons light sour cream
$^1/_2$ teaspoon paprika

- Heat the oil in a large saucepan and add the onions, potatoes and celery. Turn over in the oil and allow the vegetables to cook over a low heat for about 5 minutes.
- Add the carrots and stir for a further minute, then stir the lentils into the mixture.
- Pour in the stock, add the bay leaf, bouquet garni and seasoning. Bring to the boil slowly. Cover and simmer for about 40 minutes.
- Serve with cream drizzled over the top and shake a little paprika onto the cream and the surface of the soup.

Preparation Time: 10 minutes.
Cooking Time: 45 minutes.

Tomato & Vegetable Soup, Celery & Stilton Soup and Lentil Soup

Bean Curd Soup

the herbs, seasoning and stock; simmer for about 30 minutes.

- Remove the bouquet garni and sieve or process the soup. Serve in a heated bowl sprinkled with poppy seeds and garnished with parsley.

Preparation Time: 15 minutes.
Cooking Time: 45 minutes.

Variations
Leek and Potato Soup
Add 4 chopped leeks to the soup before adding the stock. Put through a food

Bean Curd Soup

Serves 4
4 ounces tofu, cut into cubes
1 quart vegetable stock (page 12)
Salt and pepper
4 scallions, finely chopped
6 radishes, sliced
For the garnish
Cress or parsley

- Place the tofu in the stock, season and bring to the boil. Add the onions and radishes and simmer gently for about 5 minutes.
- Divide the tofu evenly among 4 soup plates and pour on the liquid. Garnish with cress or parsley.

Preparation Time: 5 minutes.
Cooking Time: 10 minutes.

Variations
This soup can include different vegetables such as mushrooms, eggplants, snow peas, thin strips of carrot and turnip, leeks or bean

sprouts. Only use two vegetables at a time.
The tofu can also be thinly sliced, fried and drained well on kitchen paper before adding to the soup.

Potato Soup

Serves 4
2 tablespoons vegetable oil
1 large onion, finely diced
2 cloves garlic, crushed (optional)
1½ pounds peeled potatoes, sliced
1 leek, sliced (optional)
2 bay leaves, 1 bouquet garni
4 sprigs of mint, salt and pepper
6 cups vegetable stock (page 12)
For the garnish
2 teaspoons poppy seeds
Parsley sprigs

- Heat the oil in a large saucepan, add the onion and garlic and cook slowly over a low heat for about 6-8 minutes without allowing them to brown.
- Throw in the potatoes and stir round in the remaining oil. Add the leek if using. Stir in

processor or blender with 2 tablespoons cream. Garnish with cream and chopped chives. Serve hot or cold.

Potato and Pea Soup

Add 8 ounces frozen peas to the soup after simmering the potato mixture for 20 minutes. Cook for a further 15 minutes. Blend or process and serve with a swirl of cream and parsley sprigs.

Potato Soup

Cream of Carrot Soup

Cream of Carrot Soup

Serves 4
1/4 cup butter
2 medium onions, sliced
1 potato, sliced
1 pound carrots, sliced
2 stalks celery, trimmed and sliced
1 quart vegetable stock (page 12)
Salt and pepper
1 bouquet garni
1 sprig of parsley
1/2 teaspoon sugar
6 tablespoons light cream
1 teaspoon caraway seeds
For the garnish
4 sprigs mint
Wholewheat croûtons

• Heat the butter in a large saucepan and toss in the onion, potato, carrots and celery. Cook over a low heat for about 5 minutes, turning the vegetables in the butter.

• Add the stock, herbs, seasoning and sugar, then simmer for 25 minutes until the vegetables are tender. Allow to cool slightly and put through a blender or food processor.

• Reheat with the cream and caraway seeds without boiling and serve garnished with sprigs of mint and sprinkled with a few croûtons.

Preparation Time: 15 minutes.
Cooking Time: 35 minutes.

Variation
Carrot and Coriander Soup

Add 1 teaspoon ground coriander and 1/2 teaspoon cumin to the soup mixture before cooking. Blend or process, omitting the cream. Add 1 tablespoon fresh chopped coriander to the reheated soup and serve with croûtons.

Watercress Soup

Serves 4

1 pound potatoes, peeled and sliced

$^1/_2$ onion, sliced

$2^1/_2$ cups vegetable stock (page 12)

Salt and pepper

4 scallions, sliced

3 bunches watercress, washed

2 teaspoons fresh or $^1/_2$ teaspoon dried chervil

$1^1/_4$ cups milk, $^1/_4$ teaspoon nutmeg

For the garnish

4 tablespoons light cream

Fine strips of lemon or orange peel

- Cook the potatoes and onion in the stock with some seasoning for about 20 minutes until the potatoes are soft.
- Add the scallions and the watercress with the thick stalks removed. Sprinkle in the chervil and allow the soup to cook for a further 10 minutes.
- Allow to cool slightly and pass through a liquidizer or food processor.
- Reheat gently with the milk and nutmeg without boiling. Serve with a little cream in each bowl and a garnish of watercress leaves with a few strips of lemon or orange peel.

Preparation Time: 15 minutes.

Cooking Time: 35 minutes.

Variation

Lettuce Soup

Use 1 whole onion, finely diced, and 2 washed shredded lettuces in place of the watercress. Both soups can be served hot or cold.

Mushroom Soup

Serves 4

$^1/_4$ cup butter

1 small onion or 2 shallots, chopped

3 cups mushrooms, washed and chopped into small pieces

1 tablespoon all-purpose flour

1 quart vegetable stock (page 12)

1 bouquet garni, 1 bay leaf

Salt and pepper

4 tablespoon white wine

4 tablespoon light cream

For the garnish

Thinly sliced mushrooms, parsley sprigs

- Heat the butter in a large saucepan. Add the onion or shallots and stir for about 2 minutes. Toss in the mushrooms and allow to cook for another 3 minutes, stirring from time to time.

- Pour in the vegetable stock, add the bouquet garni, bay leaf, seasoning and white wine.
- Stir over a medium heat and then simmer over a low heat for about 35 minutes.
- Add the cream, stir well and serve in warm bowls garnished with mushroom slices and parsley sprigs.

Preparation Time: 15 minutes.
Cooking Time: 40 minutes.

Variation
Cream of Mushroom Soup
Use 1 pound mushrooms and $^1/_2$ cup whipping cream. Cook as above and then allow to cool slightly. Add the cream, pass through a blender or food processor and reheat gently without boiling. Garnish with sliced mushrooms and sprigs of parsley.

Golden Vegetable Soup

Serves 4
1 onion, diced, 4-5 medium carrots, diced
$^1/_2$ cup turnip, diced,
1 parsnip, diced
2 potatoes, sliced
1 leek, sliced
2 tablespoons yellow split peas, washed
1 quart vegetable stock (page 12)
Salt and pepper
$1^1/_4$ cups milk
For the garnish
Slices of cooked vegetables

- Place all the vegetables in the stock and simmer for at least 30 minutes or until the potatoes are cooked.
- Blend or process the soup, reserving some vegetables for garnish, and return to the saucepan. Add the milk and reheat gently.

Preparation Time: 15 minutes.
Cooking Time: 35 minutes.

Variations
Squash Soup
Replace the carrots with 1 pound peeled and diced squash and omit the split peas. Cook as above. Garnish with a swirl of cream and parsley sprigs

Pumpkin Soup
Replace carrots with $1^1/_2$ pounds pumpkin flesh, omitting the split peas. Season with $^1/_2$ teaspoon paprika and a good pinch of nutmeg. Add 1 teaspoon brown sugar, cook as above and garnish with cream and croûtons.

BELOW, LEFT TO RIGHT: *Watercress Soup, Mushroom Soup and Golden Vegetable Soup*

Starters and Snacks

Vegetables, both cooked and uncooked, make delicious snacks as well as interesting starters to complete meals, and are rather lighter and easier to digest than those containing meat and fish. From such evergreen favorites as avocados served with a tasty dressing, to artichokes with Hollandaise sauce – all are a delight to the eye and guaranteed to whet even the tiniest of appetites. Phyllo, puff, and short-crust pastry with savory vegetable fillings are easy to prepare as cook-ahead starters and stuffed vegetables, such as zucchini, mushrooms, small eggplants and tomatoes are all excellent, as are the popular dips for crudités and the more unusual vegetable molds and pâtés.

Mediterranean Dip

Serves 4
1 large eggplant, washed
1 small onion, finely chopped
1-2 garlic cloves, crushed
2 tablespoons olive oil
6 tablespoons thick yogurt
Salt and pepper
Juice of 1 lemon
1 tablespoon parsley, finely chopped

• Preheat the oven to 400°F.
• Prick the eggplant all over and place in the oven for about 10 minutes. Alternatively, place in the microwave for about 6 minutes.

Crudités with Mediterranean Dip and Tomato Salsa (page 27)

- Cut the peppers into even-sized strips and place in the iced water.
- Trim the scallions and cut down vertically into the green part. Place in the iced water when they will curl up to resemble flowers.
- Cut the celery into pieces the same size as the peppers and add to the bowl. Cut the carrots into strips and add to the vegetables with the mushrooms and cherry tomatoes.
- Drain well before serving and dry with kitchen paper. Arrange on an attractive dish with any favorite dip.

Preparation Time: 15 minutes.

Spicy Satay Dip

Makes about 2 cups
2 tablespoons oil
1 medium onion, finely chopped
2 cloves garlic
2 teaspoons mild curry powder
2 teaspoons cumin
2 teaspoons garam masala
2 teaspoons tomato paste
1 teaspoon mango chutney
3 tablespoons yogurt
8 ounces peanuts
1 1/4 cups canned coconut milk

- Heat the oil and cook the onion and garlic over a medium heat for about 4 minutes.
- Sprinkle in the curry powder, cumin and garam masala and fry for 1 minute. Stir briskly to form a paste. Add the tomato paste, chutney and yogurt.
- Put the peanuts and coconut milk into a food processor or blender. Switch on for a few seconds. Add the contents of the frying pan and process for a few seconds only as the mixture should be roughly chopped rather than smooth.
- This makes an excellent dip or accompaniment to vegetable kebabs such as Potato Kebabs (page 59).

Preparation Time: 10 minutes.
Cooking Time: 10 minutes.

- Allow to cool slightly, cut in half and scoop out the flesh. Mash the flesh in a bowl or place in the food processor or blender. Add the garlic and blend together.
- Gradually add the oil and then the yogurt. Season and flavour to taste with salt, pepper and lemon juice.
- Chill and serve with crudités or toast.

Preparation Time: 10 minutes.
Cooking Time: 10 minutes.

Variation
For the more traditional Greek version, omit the yogurt and add 4 teaspoons fresh white breadcrumbs. Garnish with black olives.

Crudités

Serves 4-6
1 sweet green and 1 sweet red pepper, deseeded
6 scallions
4 stalks celery, strings removed
4 medium carrots
1 small cauliflower, washed and broken into florets
4 halved mushrooms, 8 cherry tomatoes

- Wash all the vegetables thoroughly as they are to be served raw. Dry in a clean dish towel or kitchen paper. Prepare a large bowl of iced water.

Avocado Dip

Avocado Dip

Serves 4
2 ripe avocados
2 stalks celery, finely diced
4 tablespoons light cream cheese
Salt and pepper, juice of $\frac{1}{2}$ lemon
Few drops Tabasco or chili sauce
For the garnish
Celery leaves
Lemon twists

• Halve the avocados carefully, remove the
  pits and scoop out the flesh. Retain the
  skins if they are to be used as serving
  dishes – a little lemon juice in each will
  prevent discoloration. With a fork, mash the
  avocado flesh in a bowl with the diced
  celery and stir in the cream cheese. Add
  seasonings and lemon juice to taste.
• Arrange in the avocado skins or in glass
  dishes. Garnish with celery leaves or lemon
  twists.
• Serve with crudités, potato chips or toast.

Preparation Time: 10 minutes

Guacamole

Serves 4
2 ripe avocados, peeled and pitted
1-2 cloves garlic, crushed,
4 scallions, thinly sliced
2 large ripe tomatoes, skinned and chopped
1 tablespoon lemon or lime juice
1-2 chili peppers (to taste), salt and pepper

• Scrape the avocado flesh into a bowl with
  the garlic and mash together with a fork.
  Add the onions, tomatoes and lemon juice
  and mix again.
• Remove the seeds from the chilies and cut

Hummus with pitta bread and olives

into tiny pieces. Take care not to touch the eyes or face until you have washed your hands thoroughly. Wash the chopping board.

• Add the chilies to the avocado mixture with the seasoning and mix well to produce a rather lumpy appearance.

• Alternatively, place all the ingredients, apart from the tomato, in the food processor or blender and mix for a few seconds. Add the tomato and switch the machine on and off again as soon as it has mixed.

• Serve with tortilla chips or toast.

Preparation Time: 10 minutes.

Hummus

Serves 4

8 ounces canned chick peas, drained
2-3 garlic cloves, crushed
4 tablespoons olive oil
2 tablespoons tahini paste
2 tablespoons water
Juice of 1 lemon, salt and pepper

For the garnish
Black olives, $1/2$ teaspoon paprika

• Mash the beans in a bowl with the garlic and gradually work in the olive oil, tahini paste and water to a creamy consistency.

• Add the lemon juice and seasonings and serve slightly chilled with pitta bread. Alternatively, mix all the ingredients to a smoother consistency in a food processor or blender.

• Garnish with black olives and a shake of paprika.

Preparation Time: 10 minutes.

Note: If using dried chick peas, soak in cold water (see page 10). Bring to the boil in a large pan of water and simmer for 1 hour until soft.

Garlic Mushrooms

Serves 4

1 tablespoon olive oil
2 tablespoons butter
1 small onion, finely chopped
2-3 cloves garlic, crushed
1 pound small mushrooms, washed and dried
1 cup dry white wine
1/4 cup chopped parsley
1 tablespoon chopped fresh thyme
Salt and pepper

- Heat the oil and butter in a large frying pan over a medium heat and add the onion and garlic. Allow to cook for 3-4 minutes and then add the mushrooms. Cook for 5 minutes until the mushrooms have softened.
- Add the wine to the mixture and simmer on a low heat until the liquid is reduced. Stir in the parsley and thyme and season well. Serve immediately with crusty bread.

Preparation time: 8 minutes.
Cooking Time: 15 minutes.

Mushroom Bruschetta

Serves 4

2 garlic cloves, crushed
3 tablespoons olive oil
Grated rind of 1 lemon
8 large flat mushrooms, cut into quarters
4 large slices Italian bread
3-4 tablespoons Pesto Sauce (page 81)
2 tablespoons chopped parsley
Salt and pepper

- Preheat the broiler for at least 5 minutes. In a flat heatproof dish, mix the garlic, oil, and lemon rind. Turn the mushrooms around in the dish until well coated.
- Place the mushrooms under the heat and cook for about 10 minutes.
- Keep the mushrooms warm and toast one side of the bread. Spread the toasted slices with pesto sauce, top with the mushroom mixture and place under the broiler for about 4 minutes until hot.
- Serve immediately, sprinkled with parsley.

Preparation Time: 10 minutes.
Cooking Time: 15 minutes.

Mint & Yogurt Dip

Serves 4

1 1/4 cups yogurt
3 scallions, finely chopped
1/2 teaspoon fresh ginger, grated
1 clove garlic, crushed
2-3 tablespoons mint leaves, finely chopped
1 tablespoon fresh coriander, chopped
Pinch of chili powder
salt and pepper
For the garnish
Mint leaves

- Put the yogurt into a bowl and whisk slightly. Season well.
- Add all the other ingredients and mix well. Transfer into a serving dish and garnish with mint leaves. Serve as a dip for potato chips, poppadums or raw vegetables. This mixture can also be used as an accompaniment to curries.

Preparation time: 15 minutes by hand.
5 minutes in food processor.

Tomato, Cheese & Green Onion Dip

Makes 1 1/4 cups

4 tablespoons cottage cheese
1 teaspoon lemon juice
1 tablespoon tomato paste
2-3 drops Tabasco sauce
1 tablespoon light sour cream
Salt and pepper
3 tomatoes, peeled and chopped
6 scallions, finely chopped
For the garnish
Tomato rings
Scallion rings

- Mix the cheese with the lemon juice, the tomato paste, Tabasco sauce, cream and seasoning.
- Fold in the tomatoes and scallions. Pile into a dish and garnish with the tomato and scallion rings.

Preparation Time: 15 minutes.

Creamed Mushrooms

Serves 4-6

6 tablespoons butter
1/2 small onion, finely sliced
1 tablespoon olive oil
2 cloves garlic, crushed
1 1/2 pounds large mushrooms, sliced
Salt and pepper
1 1/2 cups heavy cream
1 1/2 cups Béchamel Sauce (page 35)
1 1/2 cups dry white wine
3/4 cup Parmesan cheese (grated)

- Heat the butter in a large frying pan, add the garlic and onion and cook over a moderate heat for 2 minutes without coloring.
- Add the mushrooms and cook for 10 minutes, stirring from time to time. Remove onto a plate with a slotted spoon.
- Add the wine to the pan, bring back to the boil and reduce it down to a few tablespoons.
- Add all but 2 tablespoons of the cream to the pan and continue cooking for a few minutes until the cream has thickened. Add remainder of the cream and stir well.
- Remove from the heat and stir in the Béchamel sauce. Season to taste.
- Mix with the mushroom mixture and turn into a heatproof dish. Sprinkle with the Parmesan and place dish under a hot broiler until the top has nicely browned.

Preparation Time: 5 minutes plus additional time for making Béchamel sauce.
Cooking Time: 25-30 minutes.

OPPOSITE: *Mint & Yogurt Dip (TOP) and Tomato, Cheese & Green Onion Dip*

Leeks Vinaigrette

Serves 4
8 small young leeks
1/2 cup best olive oil
2 tablespoons lemon juice
salt and pepper
For the garnish
Chopped basil or parsley
2 chopped hard boiled-eggs (optional)

• Carefully trim and clean the baby leeks.
Leaving them whole, either steam or lightly
cook them until just tender.
• Allow to cool then arrange on an oblong
dish.
• Cover with an oily vinaigrette made from
the olive oil, lemon juice, salt and white
pepper combined together.
• Cover with the finely chopped hard-boiled
eggs (if used) and garnish with the finely
chopped basil or parsley.

Preparation Time: 10 minutes .
Cooking Time: 10 minutes.

Tzatziki

Makes $1^{1}/_{4}$ cups
1 small cucumber, peeled
1-2 cloves garlic, crushed
$1^{1}/_{4}$ cups thick yogurt
1 tablespoon lemon juice
1 tablespoon finely chopped mint
Salt and pepper

• Cut the cucumber into small pieces and
mix in a bowl with the garlic, yogurt and
lemon juice.
• Stir in the mint and season to taste.

Preparation Time: 8 minutes.

To make a smooth mixture, combine the
ingredients in the food processor or blender.
Alternatively, grate the cucumber. Serve as a
dip for pitta bread.

Indian Raita is similar to Tzatziki but
with the mint omitted and perhaps a little
ground cumin added. It is served as a cooling
accompaniment to hot curries.

Dolmades

Dolmades

1 pack vacuum-packed vine leaves
2 tablespoons sunflower oil
2 medium onions, finely chopped
1 cup brown rice, cooked
¼ cup pine nuts, chopped
2 tablespoons parsley, chopped
1 tablespoon mint, chopped
2 tablespoons currants
2-3 tablespoons stock or water
Salt and pepper
Juice of 2 lemons
6 tablespoons olive oil

- Rinse the leaves and blanch them in boiling water for about 2 minutes or according to the pack instructions. Drain and thoroughly dry on kitchen paper.
- Heat the oil and cook the onions over a low heat until they are transparent, about 5 minutes.
- Add the rice and stir in the nuts, parsley, mint and currants. Season well with salt and pepper.
- Stir in a few teaspoons stock or water and allow the mixture to cook. When the rice still has a bite to it and the mixture is fairly dry, taste for seasoning. Allow to cool.
- Stretch out the vine leaves on a board and put 1 teaspoon stuffing mixture into each. Fold in the sides and near ends of the leaves over the filling. Roll away from the body to form cylinder shapes.
- Line an oiled baking dish with any left-over leaves and lay out the rolls, seam sides down. Pack close together.
- Preheat the oven to 325°F.
- Sprinkle with a layer of oil and lemon juice. You may need more depending on the size of the dish.
- Cover with aluminum foil and place a baking pan of similar size on top to weigh it down. Cook in the oven for about 1 hour.
- Allow to cool, when most of the liquid will be absorbed. Serve with a yogurt dressing.

Preparation Time: 30 minutes.
Cooking Time: 1½ hours.

Tomato Salsa

Makes 1¼ cups

½ cucumber, finely diced
1 small sweet red pepper, finely diced
1 small red onion, finely diced
2 ripe tomatoes, skinned
2 teaspoons red wine vinegar
1 tablespoon coriander,
chopped (optional)
Few drops Tabasco or hot pepper sauce
1 red chili pepper, finely diced (optional)

- Mix all the ingredients in a bowl and stir before serving.
- For a more interesting texture, place half the ingredients in the food processor or blender for a few seconds, then mix with the remaining chopped ingredients. Serve with tortillas or to add a little spice to vegetable rissoles or croquettes.

Preparation Time: 8 minutes.

Carrot Pâté

Serves 4

1 pound carrots, scraped and cut
into rings
4 ounces young turnip, cut into
even-sized pieces
1 yellow sweet pepper, deseeded and
cut into strips
6 tablespoons low fat yogurt
Rind and juice of 1 lemon
Salt and pepper
1 tablespoon chopped fresh dill

- Cook the carrot and turnip in boiling salted water for about 15 minutes until tender. Add the pepper for the last 5 minutes of cooking.
- Drain and cool the vegetables.
- Put into a food processor or blender with the yogurt, ½ teaspoon lemon rind, the lemon juice and seasoning; mix well until smooth. Add the dill and switch on for a second to blend.

- Turn into ramekins and chill for 30 minutes before serving with wholewheat or Melba toast.

Preparation Time: 10 minutes, plus 30 minutes chilling time.
Cooking Time: 15 minutes.

Carrot Pâté

Mozzarella & Tomatoes

Serves 4

4 large ripe tomatoes, skinned
8 ounces Mozzarella, cut into thin slices
12 basil leaves, chopped
1 teaspoon fresh oregano
Salt and pepper
4 tablespoons olive oil
1 tablespoon capers (optional)
Black olives (optional)

- Slice the tomatoes into thick rings. Cut the Mozzarella into slices of the same size.
- Arrange the slices in an overlapping pattern and sprinkle with the basil. Sprinkle on the olive oil and, if using, arrange the capers and olives on top.
- Decorate with the basil leaves and serve with crusty bread.

Preparation Time: 10 minutes.
Cooking Time: 10 minutes if serving hot.

Variation
This can be arranged on focaccia bread and can even be made into a hot starter. Drizzle some of the oil onto a round of focaccia bread and sprinkle with the basil. Arrange the tomatoes and cheese as above and put into a hot oven for about 10 minutes or until the cheese begins to run.

Celeriac Salad

Serves 6

1 large celery root (celeriac)
$\frac{1}{2}$ cup Mayonnaise (page 35) or
$\frac{1}{2}$ cup Mustard Vinaigrette (page 38)

- Peel, wash and coarsely grate the celeriac.
- Blanch in salted water for about 10 minutes to help remove the slight bitterness.
- Drain and blot dry with kitchen paper. Mix with the mayonnaise or vinaigrette and allow to chill thoroughly before serving.

Preparation Time: 10 minutes excluding chilling time.

Tapénade with Crostini

Serves 6

1 cup black olives, pitted
2 tablespoons capers, drained
1 tablespoon brandy
1 clove garlic, crushed
1 tablespoon olive oil
$\frac{1}{2}$ teaspoon chopped fresh thyme
1 tablespoon lemon juice
2 tablespoons breadcrumbs
Freshly ground black pepper
1 ciabatta loaf

- Put the olives, capers, brandy and garlic in a food processor or blender. Switch on for a few seconds to mix. Add the oil, thyme, lemon juice, breadcrumbs and a good shake of pepper. Switch on for a few seconds to mix without making it into a liquid. Turn into a dish.
- Preheat the oven to 400°F.
- Cut the bread into $\frac{1}{2}$-inch slices and spread on a baking sheet. When just beginning to brown, remove, spread on the olive mixture and serve immediately.

Preparation Time: 10 minutes.
Cooking Time: 10 minutes.

Marinated Pepper Strips

Serves 4

4-5 sweet peppers, red, green and yellow
2 cloves garlic, crushed
$^2/_3$ cup olive oil
Salt and pepper
1 chili pepper, finely chopped (optional)
2 tablespoons chopped parsley

- Preheat the broiler to high and place the peppers under it on a flat heatproof dish. Allow the peppers to char and blister, turning them around to expose all surfaces

to the heat. Place in a covered dish to cool.
- Place the garlic and seasoning into a jug with the olive oil and stir vigorously, adding the chili pepper, if liked.
- Peel the peppers, removing the thin skin and charred pieces. Cut in half and remove seeds and stalks. Cut into strips and arrange in a dish. Drizzle with oil and sprinkle with parsley.
- Leave to marinate in the refrigerator for 1-3 hours before serving with crusty rolls or chunks of wholegrain bread.

Preparation Time: 20 minutes plus 3 hours marinating time.
Cooking Time: 15 minutes.

Tofu Pâté

Serves 4

1 tablespoon chopped parsley
2 scallions, finely chopped
7-ounce pack smoked tofu
2 tablespoons lemon juice
1 garlic clove, crushed
1-2 tablespoons olive oil
Salt and pepper
$^1/_4$ teaspoon cayenne pepper
For the garnish
4 lemon slices
4 sprigs parsley
Fingers of toast

- Chop the parsley in a blender or food processor and tip it into a bowl. Next add the scallions to the goblet and chop roughly.
- Gradually add the tofu, lemon juice, garlic and olive oil.
- Season well and return the parsley for a final brief mix. Turn into a dish and garnish with the lemon wedges and parsley.

Preparation Time: 10 minutes.

If preparing by hand, chop the scallions and crush the garlic finely and cream all the ingredients together in a bowl.

Mozzarella & Tomatoes on focaccia bread

Variation
Red Pepper Tofu Pâté
Blanch a small sweet red pepper, deseeded and cut into strips, in boiling salted water for 4 minutes, drain and cool. Add to the blender or mixer with the scallions.

Italian Spiced Olives

Serves 4

$1^1/_2$ cups black olives, pitted
2 cloves garlic, crushed
1 chili pepper
4 tablespoons olive oil
2 stalks crisp celery, strings removed
2 scallions, finely chopped
1 tablespoon chopped parsley

- Place the olives in a serving bowl. Mix the garlic and chili pepper with half the oil.
- Chop the celery finely and mix with the olive oil and garlic/chili mixture.
- Add the scallions and mix well together with the remaining oil. Allow to marinate for at least one hour before serving as part of a starter.
- Sprinkle with parsley and serve with Mozzarella & Tomatoes or Marinated Pepper Strips (see above).

Preparation Time: 7 minutes.

Spanikopitta

Serves 4

1 tablespoon olive oil
1 small onion, finely chopped
8 ounces frozen spinach, thawed
4 ounces feta cheese
$^1/_4$ teaspoon nutmeg
Salt and pepper
1 egg, beaten
8 ounces wholewheat pastry (pages 94-95)
Melted butter

- Heat the oil in a pan and cook the onion over a low heat until transparent, about 4-5 minutes.
- Cook the spinach for 4 minutes in boiling salted water and drain thoroughly. Roughly chop. Put the spinach in a bowl with the

crumbled feta cheese, nutmeg, salt and pepper. Add the onion and mix well with the beaten egg.

• Oil 2 baking sheets and preheat the oven to 400°F.
• Roll the pastry out into a thin sheet of about 10 x 10 inches. Cut into quarters and divide the mixture between the four squares, rolling them over to form triangles. Crimp the edges to seal and brush over with the melted butter.
• Bake in the oven until golden brown.

Preparation Time: 40 minutes.
Cooking Time: 30 minutes.

Variations
Phyllo pastry can also be used for this recipe in which case you will need 6 sheets which can be bought ready-made.
• Cut the sheets into strips 3 inches wide and keep them covered with a damp cloth until you need them, to prevent them drying out.
• Brush one strip of pastry with melted butter and place 1 teaspoon filling mixture

Spanikopitta

at one end of the strip. Fold one corner of the pastry over the filling to form a triangle, then keep folding the angle over and over until the end of the strip is reached which should be tucked in.
• Brush the triangles with melted butter and place them seam sides down on baking sheets. Bake in the oven at 350F for 30 minutes or until golden brown and crisp.

An alternative filling is the one for Tasty Pasties on page 100.

Onion Bhaji

Makes 6

3 rounded teaspoon gram
(chick pea) flour
$\frac{1}{2}$ teaspoon cumin
$\frac{1}{2}$ teaspoon turmeric
$\frac{1}{2}$ teaspoon garam masala
1 large onion,
cut into thin rings
Oil for frying

• Mix the flour with the spices and then add the onion rings. Gradually add a little cold water until the whole mixture binds together.

• Heat the oil to 350°F or until a bread cube, when dropped in, immediately rises.

• Make the onion mixture into balls and allow to cook in the hot fat for about 4-5 minutes until golden brown. Drain on kitchen paper.

Preparation Time: 5 minutes.
Cooking Time: 10 minutes.

Vegetable Terrine

Serves 4-8

8 ounces carrots, thinly sliced
2 ounces green beans
1 sweet red pepper, deseeded and sliced
8 ounces leeks, sliced, 1 tablespoon butter
1 cup button mushrooms, sliced
2 teaspoons agar, 1 cup grated cheese
$\frac{1}{2}$ pint whipping cream
5 egg yolks, salt and pepper

• Preheat the oven to 325°F. Oil the inside of a 1-pound loaf tin.

• Cook the vegetables (except the mushrooms) lightly in separate batches in boiling water, by steaming, or in the microwave – but make sure they are crisp and not soggy. Drain well.

• Heat the butter and gently fry the mushrooms for about 3 minutes. Drain on kitchen paper and season well.

• Arrange the vegetables in layers in the loaf tin with the cheese sprinkled in between. Make up the agar in 2 teaspoons boiling water and make sure it is dissolved.

• Mix the cream, egg yolks, salt, pepper and nutmeg together. Stir in the agar and pour the mixture over the vegetables, allowing it to seep between the layers.

• Cover with foil and bake in the oven for 1 hour until the mixture comes away easily from the sides of the tin.

• Chill in the refrigerator for at least 3 hours before turning out onto a plate.

• Cut into slices and serve with a little Tomato Coulis (page 38).

Preparation Time: 30 minutes.
Cooking Time: 1 $\frac{1}{2}$ hours.

Onion Bhaji

Falafel

Makes about 16

8 ounces chick peas, canned or dried
2 onions, finely chopped
2 cloves garlic, crushed
1 teaspoon ground coriander
1 tablespoon fresh coriander, chopped
(optional)
2 teaspoons aniseed
2 teaspoons caraway seeds,
1 tablespoon parsley
Salt and pepper
1 teaspoon dried yeast
2-3 tablespoons water
2 egg whites, lightly beaten
2 cups fresh breadcrumbs
Oil for frying

- Drain the canned chick peas (see page 10 for dried) and allow to dry on kitchen paper. Put through a food processor or mincer with the onions and garlic.
- Add all the spices and herbs and mix well in the processor. Add the yeast dissolved in a little warm water. Mix with a little more water if necessary to make a stiff mixture and allow to cool in the refrigerator.
- Roll the mixture into small balls. Dip each one in the egg white and breadcrumbs and repeat. If possible, chill again before frying in hot oil until crisp.
- Serve with Mint and Yogurt Dip (page 24) or Tomato Salsa (page 27) and crisp salads.

Preparation time: 10 minutes.
Cooking time: 4 minutes for frying each batch. An extra hour will be needed for cooking dried chick peas.

Grapefruit & Melon Appetizer

Serves 4

1 tablespoons sugar (optional)
1 medium-sized ripe cantaloupe melon
2 grapefruits
For the decoration
Mint leaves

- For a sweeter appetizer, simmer the sugar in 2-3 tablespoons water and allow to cool.
- Cut the top from the melon and remove the seeds. With a melon baller, scoop out little balls into a bowl without breaking the skin of the melon. Alternatively, remove the flesh and chop it into pieces.
- With a serrated knife, peel the grapefruit from top to bottom, removing the white pith with the skin. Cut in between the segments to release the flesh leaving the skin behind. Do all this over the bowl to ensure that all the juice is saved.
- If using the sugar syrup, add to the bowl. Mix well and pile the fruit back into the melon shell. Chill before serving.

Preparation Time: 15 minutes.

Variation
Florida Cocktail
For 4 servings you will need 6 oranges and 3 grapefruits. Prepare the fruit in the same way as the grapefruit in the recipe above. Add 1-2 tablespoons sugar syrup, if preferred; however, many people enjoy the natural flavor of the fruit without additional sweetness. Arrange the different fruit segments alternately and garnish with mint and finely grated orange peel.

Stuffed Onions

Serves 4

4 medium onions, skinned
3 tablespoons olive oil
2 cloves garlic, crushed
2 pieces sun-dried tomato, chopped
1 cup cooked spinach
$1/2$ cup fresh breadcrumbs
$1/2$ cup goat's cheese
2 teaspoons fresh thyme
Salt and pepper

- Heat the oven to 400°F. Slice 1 inch from the top of the onion and remove the roots. Remove the centers of the onions and chop finely.
- Bring a large pan of salted water to the boil and add the hollowed-out onions. Cook for about 10 minutes. Remove carefully and drain upside down in a colander.
- Heat two-thirds of the oil in a pan and add the chopped onion with the tomatoes and other ingredients. Mix well.

Grapefruit & Melon Appetizer

- Stuff the onions with the mixture and place on an oiled baking sheet. Cook for 30 minutes re-painting with oil from time to time.

Preparation Time: 15 minutes.
Cooking Time: 50 minutes.

Stuffed Tomatoes

Serves 4
8 medium ripe tomatoes
1 cup wholewheat breadcrumbs
4 stalks celery, finely chopped
2 scallions, finely chopped
$^1/_4$ cup chopped walnuts
Salt and pepper

- Preheat oven to 350F.
- Cut a slice from the stem end of each tomato and retain as a lid.
- Scrape the insides of the tomatoes into a bowl leaving the shells intact.
- Finely chop the celery or cut into very small dice and add to the tomatoes. Add the remaining ingredients and mix well.
- Pile into the tomato shells with a teaspoon and place the lid on top. Place in an ovenproof dish and bake for 20 minutes or until tomatoes are soft.

Preparation Time: 10 minutes.
Cooking Time: 20 minutes.

Spicy Stuffed Zucchini

Serves 4
4 zucchini, washed
Salt and pepper, 1 tablespoon lemon juice
$^1/_2$ cup vegetable oil,
1 onion, finely diced
1 sweet red pepper, deseeded and diced
1-2 cloves garlic, crushed
2 tomatoes, skinned and chopped
1-2 teaspoons curry powder
1 cup mushrooms, finely chopped
$^1/_2$ cup long-grain rice, cooked
$^1/_2$ teaspoon paprika
1 tablespoon chopped parsley

- Put the zucchini into a pan of boiling salted water for 4 minutes (5 minutes if very thick). Drain into a colander and allow to cool slightly.
- Heat the oil in a pan, add the onion, and allow to cook on a low heat for 3 minutes. Add the pepper and the garlic and continue cooking for 3 minutes, stirring from time to time.
- Preheat the oven to 350°F.
- Cut the zucchini in half lengthwise and scoop out the flesh from the centre with a sharp knife. Arrange the shells, brushed on the outside with oil, on an oiled baking sheet. Chop the flesh and add to the onion mixture with the tomatoes. Mix well.
- Sprinkle the mixture in the pan with the curry powder. Add the mushrooms, sprinkle with pepper and finally stir in the rice.
- Arrange the filling in the zucchini shells and brush the top with oil. Cook in the oven for 20 minutes.

Preparation Time: 20 minutes.
Cooking Time: 35 minutes.

Stuffed Tomatoes

Sauces

A delicious sauce will greatly enhance almost any dish. This is especially true of vegetables. Think of globe artichokes, for example, served with a velvety Hollandaise sauce to make a tempting and unusual first course. A dish of lightly steamed cauliflower or broccoli will be dramatically improved by a good cheese or parsley sauce and a tomato sauce or coulis makes an excellent accompaniment to stuffed vegetables, vegetable terrines, pastas and rice dishes.

Basic White Sauce

Basic White Sauce

Coating sauce

Makes $2\frac{1}{2}$ cups
$\frac{1}{4}$ cup butter or margarine
$\frac{1}{4}$ cup all-purpose flour
Salt and pepper, $2\frac{1}{2}$ cups milk

- Melt the butter in a saucepan over a medium heat. Remove from the heat and stir in the flour. When smooth, gradually add the milk away from the heat, beating all the time until the mixture is smooth.
- Season well and cook over a gentle heat, whisking or beating with a wooden spoon until the sauce has thickened.

Preparation Time: 5 minutes.
Cooking Time: 10 minutes.

Pouring sauce

This will only require 2 tablespoons butter or margarine and the same of flour to $2\frac{1}{2}$ cups milk.

Binding sauce

This will require $\frac{1}{4}$ cup butter or margarine and $\frac{1}{4}$ cup all-purpose flour to $2\frac{1}{4}$ cups milk. Use for rissoles and quenelles.

Variations

Use either a Basic White Sauce or a Béchamel Sauce as a base for these:

Cheese sauce

Add $\frac{1}{2}$ cup grated cheese, $\frac{1}{2}$ teaspoon dry mustard and $\frac{1}{2}$ teaspoon paprika to $1\frac{1}{4}$ cups coating sauce.

Caper sauce

Add 1 tablespoon finely chopped capers and 1 teaspoon of the caper liquid to $1\frac{1}{4}$ cups sauce.

Parsley sauce

Add 2 tablespoons chopped parsley to $1\frac{1}{4}$ cups sauce.

Sour cream sauce

Add 4 tablespoons light sour cream to $1\frac{1}{4}$ cups sauce (1 teaspoon lemon rind can be added).

Egg sauce

Add 2 chopped hard-boiled eggs and 1 tablespoon chopped chives to $1\frac{1}{4}$ cups sauce.

Mushroom sauce

Add 1 cup chopped mushrooms cooked in 1 tablespoon of butter to $1\frac{1}{4}$ cups sauce to which $\frac{1}{2}$ teaspoon paprika has been added.

Béchamel Sauce

This is a flavored white sauce and it is well worth the extra time making it as it tastes infinitely superior to a basic white sauce. The flour must be added away from the heat or the starch grains will burst causing lumps to form in the sauce.

Makes $2\frac{1}{2}$ cups
$2\frac{1}{2}$ cups milk
1 small onion, cut into slices
1 carrot, sliced
6 slightly crushed peppercorns
1 blade mace
1 sprig parsley
1 bay leaf
$\frac{1}{4}$ *cup butter or margarine*
$\frac{1}{4}$ *cup all-purpose flour*
Salt and pepper

• Pour the milk into a saucepan and add the onion, carrot, peppercorns and herbs. Bring to the boil and simmer gently over a low heat for 15 minutes. To avoid sticking, it is best to put the milk in a double boiler or in a heatproof bowl over hot water. Allow to cool, leaving the vegetables in the milk. Strain and make the milk up to $2\frac{1}{2}$ cups with vegetable stock or more milk.
• Heat the butter or margarine in a saucepan, remove from the heat and add the flour to make a *roux* (term for melted fat mixed with flour). Stir well until smooth and well blended.
• Add the strained milk (off the heat) and whisk or beat well with a wooden spoon to avoid lumps. When the sauce is smooth, season, return to the heat and cook for about 4-5 minutes, stirring well to make sure the sauce is lump-free. Taste for seasoning and to make sure that the flour is cooked.
• Use to coat vegetables, to mix with vegetable gratins and to serve in pasta dishes such as lasagna and cannelloni. A thicker version of this sauce can be used to bind mixtures for croquettes and rissoles.

Preparation Time: 10 minutes plus 20 minutes infusing time.
Cooking Time: 10-15 minutes.

Mayonnaise

Makes $\frac{2}{3}$ cup
2 egg yolks
$\frac{1}{4}$ *teaspoon salt*
$\frac{1}{4}$ *teaspoon sugar*
$\frac{1}{2}$ *teaspoon French mustard*
$\frac{1}{2}$ *cup olive oil*
1 tablespoon white wine vinegar

• Stand a small bowl on a towel to prevent slipping. Tip in the egg yolks (which must be at room temperature), salt, sugar and mustard. Mix together with a small wooden spoon or an electric hand mixer.
• Add the oil drop by drop, stirring vigorously all the time; as the oil is added, the mixture should become thick. If the mixture becomes too thick, add a little vinegar and continue stirring and adding the oil. When all the ingredients are incorporated, taste for seasoning. The mixture should be thick and creamy.

Preparation Time: 10 minutes.

Variation
• To make mayonnaise quickly in the blender or food processor, use a whole egg which must be at room temperature and not straight from the refrigerator. Put the egg into the blender or food processor with salt, pepper and a drop of vinegar and process for a few seconds.
• Add up to $1\frac{1}{4}$ cups olive oil very slowly, while the machine is running, until the mixture is thick. Add the remaining vinegar or lemon juice to taste.

Preparation Time: 10 minutes by hand, 5 minutes by machine.

Béchamel Sauce

Herb Mayonnaise

Add 1-2 tablespoons chopped parsley, chives or chervil to the basic mayonnaise.

Garlic Mayonnaise (Aïoli)

1-4 cloves of crushed garlic can be added when making the mayonnaise and before the oil. Serve with Crudités (page 21).

Russian Dressing

Add 1 tablespoon tomato ketchup, 1 teaspoon grated horseradish, 3-4 drops Tabasco or chili sauce, 2 finely chopped scallions, 2 tablespoons chopped gherkins to the basic mayonnaise.

Tomato Mayonnaise

Add 2 tablespoons tomato paste to the mayonnaise, an extra $\frac{1}{2}$ teaspoon lemon juice and a few drops of Tabasco sauce. Good in vegetable salads.

Use mayonnaise as a dressing for salads, for coating hard-boiled eggs, mixing with pasta and vegetable salads.

Basic Tomato Sauce

Makes $2\frac{1}{2}$ cups

2 tablespoons oil, 1 onion, diced
2 stalks celery, sliced
1 carrot grated
$2\frac{1}{2}$ cups canned tomato purée
(sieved tomatoes)
6 basil leaves, $\frac{1}{2}$ teaspoon thyme
1 bay leaf, salt and pepper

• Heat the oil in a saucepan, add the onion and cook over a low heat for 4 minutes. Add the celery and carrot and cook for a further 4 minutes.

• Add all the ingredients and 8 tablespoons water. Season well, bring to the boil, reduce the heat and simmer for 30 minutes.

• Sieve, or pass through a blender or food processor. Use as required with pasta, rice dishes or for stuffed vegetables.

It is a good idea to make up large quantities of this sauce from fresh tomatoes, when they are cheap and plentiful, and freeze portions for future use.

Preparation Time: 10 minutes.
Cooking Time: 40 minutes.

Basic Tomato Sauce

Hollandaise Sauce

Makes $^2/_3$ cup
2 egg yolks
2 teaspoons lemon juice
$^1/_2$ cup unsalted butter
Salt

- Rest a small bowl on top of a saucepan of boiling water, making sure the base is not touching the water, and add the egg yolks and lemon juice, stirring them together.
- Cut the butter into small pieces and add them gradually, stirring constantly until the sauce is thick. If the mixture starts to curdle and resemble scrambled eggs, remove from the heat and whisk in 1 teaspoon cold water.
- Continue cooking until all the butter is incorporated. Serve at once as this sauce tends to separate as it cools.

Good with steamed or boiled vegetables such as asparagus, broccoli, leeks, as well as white fish, shellfish and salmon.

Preparation Time: 5 minutes.
Cooking Time: 8 minutes.

To make the sauce in a blender or food processor
- Heat the butter with 1 tablespoon water and 1 teaspoon wine vinegar until melted but not browned.
- Put the egg yolks into the blender or food processor, switch on to minimum speed and pour the butter in slowly. The sauce should thicken. Add a little salt and pepper with the lemon juice for flavoring. If the sauce is too thin, put it in the microwave for about 5 seconds and whisk until thick. Alternatively put in a bowl over hot water and whisk until thick.

Variation
Mousseline sauce
Make up the Hollandaise sauce.
- Add 4 tablespoons heavy cream to the sauce. Whisk until smooth and serve warm immediately. This sauce can be stored in the refrigerator and served cold or can be gently re-heated over warm water. Serve with green vegetables, eggs or fish.

Orange Hollandaise
Add 1 tablespoon fresh orange juice instead of the lemon juice and vinegar.

Add a little grated rind to the sauce and garnish with blanched strips of orange peel. Leeks and broccoli combine particularly well with the flavor of oranges.

ABOVE: *Orange Hollandaise*

BELOW: *Hollandaise Sauce*

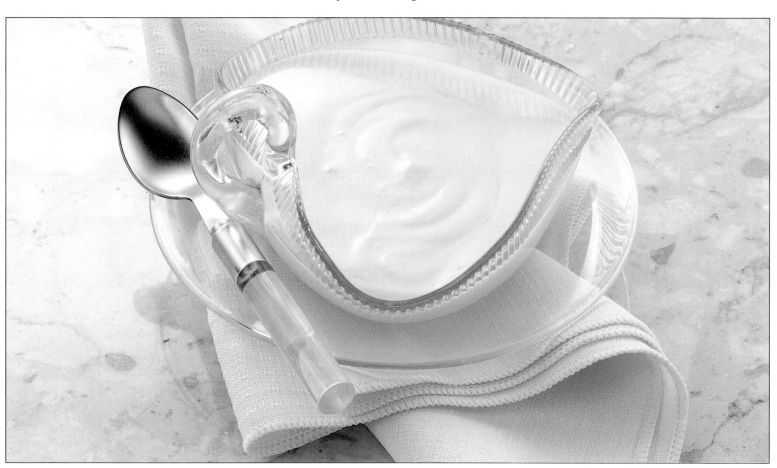

Tomato Coulis

Makes 1¼ cups
1 pound ripe tomatoes, skinned
1 tablespoon chopped parsley
1 tablespoon chopped basil
1 teaspoon lemon juice
½ teaspoon sugar
Salt and pepper

- Halve the tomatoes and allow them to drain in a sieve for 30 minutes. Remove the seeds and chop the flesh into small dice.
- Add all the other ingredients, stirring together gently, and allow to stand for 1 hour in the refrigerator. Serve with cold vegetable dishes such as the Vegetable Terrine on page 31.
- The coulis can be passed through a fine sieve to make a thin, smooth sauce to add color and freshness to other dishes.

Preparation Time: 20 minutes.

Sweet Pepper Sauce

Makes 2½ cups
1 sweet red, 1 green
1 yellow pepper,
halved and deseeded
1 teaspoon olive oil
2 cups Tomato Sauce (page 36)
6 basil leaves, chopped
1 tablespoon parsley

- Preheat the broiler. Prepare the peppers and lay them, skins uppermost, on a flat heatproof dish. Paint them all over with oil before placing under the heat.
- After 4-5 minutes, turn the peppers over and paint with the oil again. Return to the heat for another 5 minutes.
- Allow to cool slightly and remove the thin skin from the peppers. Cut into strips and then into dice.
- Mix the peppers with the tomato sauce, the basil and parsley. Reheat as required but do not boil or the flavor will be impaired. Serve with pasta or with stuffed vegetables.

Preparation time: 15 minutes.
Cooking Time: 40 minutes.

Basic Vinaigrette

Makes ⅔ cup
6 tablespoons olive oil
¼ teaspoon salt
White pepper
¼ teaspoon superfine sugar
2 tablespoons white wine vinegar or lemon juice

- Put all the ingredients in a screw-top jar and shake vigorously. Use as required on salads and vegetables.

Preparation Time: 3 minutes.

If storing the dressing in the refrigerator allow 1 hour for it to come back to room temperature. Shake the bottle well to mix.

Variation
Mustard Vinaigrette
Add ¼ teaspoon French mustard to the Basic Vinaigrette and shake well.

Garlic Dressing
Slightly crush 1 large garlic clove. Add to the Vinaigrette. Shake well and allow to stand for 12 hours before removing garlic (optional).

Blue Cheese Dressing
Add 1 ounce Stilton, Roquefort or Danish Blue cheese to the Basic Vinaigrette dressing.

Green Dressing
Add a tablespoon each of chopped parsley, scallions or capers to the Garlic Dressing. A tablespoon each of chopped basil and parsley tastes good with tomato salads.

ABOVE: *Green Dressing*

RIGHT: *Mustard Vinaigrette, Herb Mayonnaise (page 36) and the classic Vinaigrette with herbs*

Sweet Corn Relish

Makes 1 quart

1 pound frozen or canned corn, drained
2 stalks celery, finely sliced
2 sweet red peppers, deseeded and diced
1 onion, chopped
$^2/_3$ cup pickling vinegar
2 tablespoons sugar
1 teaspoon salt
$^1/_2$ teaspoon celery seeds
1 tablespoon all-purpose flour
1 teaspoon dry mustard
$^1/_4$ teaspoon turmeric

- Put the corn in a large saucepan with $^2/_3$ cup water over a low heat. Add the celery, red peppers, onion and simmer for 5 minutes.
- Pour in the vinegar, add the sugar, salt and celery seeds, stir and bring to the boil. Keep the mixture on the boil for 10 minutes.
- Wash some jelly jars and place them in a low oven for 20 minutes to sterilize them.
- Mix the flour, mustard and turmeric together and blend into a smooth paste with a little cold water. Add some of the hot pickle to the paste and then return all the mixture to the saucepan. Stir vigorously until the mixture comes back to the boil and is bubbling. Simmer for 5 minutes.
- Ladle into the hot, sterilized jars and cover.

Preparation Time: 30 minutes.
Cooking Time: 20 minutes.

Variation

6 fresh corn cobs can be used. Carefully remove the corn from the cob using a sharp knife. Cook for 10 minutes before adding the other ingredients.

Tofu Dressing

Makes 1$^1/_4$ cups

10 ounces silken tofu
2 tablespoons lemon juice
2 tablespoons sunflower oil
1 crushed clove garlic

- Put all the ingredients in the blender or food processor and mix together until creamy.
- Use this dressing on salads. It is a healthy low calorie option to mayonnaise and other oily dressings.

Preparation Time: 5 minutes.

Variation

Add 1 teaspoon soy sauce or chili sauce for a hotter dressing for rissoles and veggie burgers.

Sweet Corn Relish

Barbecue Sauce

Barbecue Sauce

Makes 1$\frac{1}{2}$ cups
2 tablespoons butter or margarine
1 onion, finely chopped
1 garlic clove, crushed
1 green and 1 red sweet pepper,
cut into chunks
2 tablespoons wine vinegar
1$\frac{2}{3}$ cups stock or water
1 tablespoon French mustard
2 tablespoons brown sugar
1 slice of lemon
1 bay leaf
$\frac{1}{4}$ teaspoon cayenne pepper
6 tablespoons ketchup or home-made
Tomato Sauce (page 36)
2 tablespoons tomato paste
Salt and pepper

- Heat the butter or margarine in a medium-sized pan and cook the onions, peppers and garlic for 4 minutes without browning.
- Add all the remaining ingredients and stir well. Bring to the boil and simmer for about 15 minutes, stirring from time to time. Remove the lemon slice and bay leaf before pouring into a jug. Serve with kebabs or Lentil & Peanut Burgers (page 65).

Preparation Time: 10 minutes.
Cooking Time: 25 minutes.

Main Courses

Vegetarian main courses are usually a combination of several dishes. Eggs cooked in various ways are delicious with salads, while pasta combines well with vegetables as well as cheeses. Rice can accompany many dishes as well as combining with other ingredients to make nutritious and substantial stuffings for vegetables.

These days people are traveling more and more widely, so it is little wonder that foreign influences continue to creep in, providing new inspiration for healthy and different ways with food. The concept of eating several dishes together, as in Greek, Indian, Chinese, Thai and Japanese cultures, is of great appeal to vegetarians as well as intoducing a diversity of flavors and nutriments to their diet.

Food should look attractive in order to appeal first of all to the eye and some thought should also be given to color and texture when preparing it. However delicious they may be individually, three gratin dishes served together at the same meal can soon begin to pall. One dish with a colorful sauce, another with crisp vegetables, a third composed of fresh salads or fruits is a far more appetizing choice.

and sprinkle with the cheese, breadcrumbs and half the parsley. Cook for a further 25 minutes and sprinkle with the remaining parsley before serving.

Preparation Time: 30 minutes.
Cooking Time: 1$\frac{1}{2}$ hours.

Variation
Mixed Vegetable Bake
Line the bottom of the dish with 1 cup cooked green lentils. Deseed and chop into strips 1sweet red and 1 sweet green pepper.

Eggplant Bake

Serves 4

2 large eggplants, sliced
4 zucchini, sliced
6-8 tablespoons olive oil
2 medium onions, thinly sliced
1 cup mushrooms
1 16-ounce can plum tomatoes or
2 pounds fresh plum tomatoes
Salt and pepper
1 teaspoon oregano
$\frac{1}{2}$ teaspoon chili sauce
2 large potatoes, thinly sliced
2 tablespoons butter
or margarine
4 tablespoons light cream
For the topping
$\frac{1}{2}$ cup grated cheese
2 tablespoons fresh breadcrumbs
2 tablespoons chopped parsley

- Arrange the $\frac{1}{2}$-inch slices of eggplant on a plastic tray or a baking sheet and sprinkle with salt. Allow to stand for about 30 minutes. Treat the zucchini in the same way. Wipe dry with kitchen paper, or if cutting down on salt, rinse and dry.
- Heat 2 tablespoons of oil in a large pan and cook the onions on a low heat until transparent. Remove half into a wide and shallow ovenproof dish and the other half onto a plate.
- Heat the remaining oil and lightly fry the eggplants, zucchini and mushrooms in batches, placing each one into the dish and layering with the remaining onions. Add the tomatoes, seasoning and herbs. Spread the cream over the top.
- Pre-heat the oven to 400°F.
- Top with the sliced potatoes and brush with melted butter or margarine.
- Bake in the oven for 40 minutes. Remove

Slices of eggplant, tomato and mushrooms can be arranged in layers along with the pepper strips.

Pour 2$\frac{1}{2}$ cups Béchamel Sauce (page 35) over the top layer of vegetables and continue with the topping as in the previous recipe.

Serve with garlic bread, extra cheese and a mixed green salad.

Mixed Vegetable Bake

Roasted Vegetables

Serves 4

4 medium potatoes, peeled
4 small parsnips, scraped
6 tablespoons olive oil
4 red onions, quartered
4 zucchini, halved
1 sweet green and 1 red pepper, deseeded and quartered
4 plum tomatoes, halved or 2 large ripe tomatoes, quartered
4 sprigs rosemary
4-6 cloves garlic, unpeeled
salt

- Cut the potatoes into even-sized pieces and place in salted water with the parsnips, which should be halved lengthways. Bring to the boil and cook for 7 minutes. Drain in a colander and shake well, roughing up the outsides of the vegetables. Alternatively, scratch them all over with a fork.
- Preheat the oven to 425°F. Rub oil all over a large roasting tin or ovenproof dish.
- Arrange the potatoes, parsnips and onions in the roasting tin. Place the zucchini, peppers and tomatoes between the root vegetables. Spread the herbs and garlic at intervals among the vegetables.
- Brush the vegetables with the oil, making sure they are covered and then drizzle the remainder over them. Sprinkle with salt (sea salt is best).
- Place in the oven for 20 minutes. Remove, baste and turn the vegetables, then return for a further 25 minutes or until the vegetables are tender. Serve hot with the pan juices and a basket of wholewheat bread for mopping them up. These vegetables are delicious served with pasta or rice.

Preparation Time: 20 minutes.
Cooking Time: 1 hour.

Variation
The Mediterranean combination of eggplant slices, halved fennel heads and halved endives can be roasted without pre-cooking together with tiny onions, cherry tomatoes, sweet peppers and plenty of garlic, the cloves of which can be left whole.

Eggplant & Zucchini Fritters

Serves 4

2 eggplants, sliced lengthways
4 zucchini, cut into $\frac{1}{2}$-inch rounds
Salt
For the batter
1 cup all-purpose flour
1 teaspoon baking powder
1 egg
1 tablespoon olive oil
$\frac{2}{3}$ cup water
1 teaspoon dried oregano
1 lemon, cut into wedges
Oil for frying

- Sprinkle the sliced eggplants with salt and allow to stand for about 30 minutes on a tray or in a colander. Treat the zucchini in the same way.
- Sift the flour into a bowl with the baking powder. Make a well in the center, then add the egg and the oil with a little of the water and herbs. Whisk until smooth, adding the remaining water gradually.
- Rinse the salt away from the eggplant and zucchini and dry with kitchen paper.
- Heat a frying pan half filled with oil (preferably olive for flavor). Test by throwing a cube of bread into the oil. If it browns and comes to the surface immediately, start frying the fritters.
- Spear a piece of vegetable on a fork, dip it into the batter, then lift and allow the excess to drain back into the bowl. Place carefully into the oil. Fry no more than 4 pieces at one time. Remove with a slotted spoon, drain on kitchen paper and keep warm.
- Garnish each serving with wedges of lemon.

Preparation Time: 30 minutes.
Cooking Time: 20 minutes.

Variation
Sweet Potato Fritters
Boil 3 sweet potatoes until just tender and drain well. Slice, dip in batter and fry as for eggplant and zucchini. Allow a cooking time that is longer by about 2-3 minutes.

Grilled Italian Vegetables

Serves 4

3 eggplants, cut into thick rings
6 zucchini, cut into rounds, salt
24 small button mushrooms
6 tablespoons olive oil
2 sweet red and 2 yellow pepper,
deseeded and cut into thick slices
1 tablespoon chopped rosemary

• Sprinkle the eggplants and zucchini with salt and allow to stand in colanders or on plastic trays for about 30 minutes. Rinse off the salt and dry with kitchen paper.
• Pour the oil into a shallow dish and stand the eggplants and zucchini in the oil for 5 minutes, turning once.
• Meanwhile, slice the peppers and paint all

Grilled Italian Vegetables

over with the oil from the dish. Do the same with the mushrooms.
• Grill over a barbecue or preheat a lightly oiled heavy iron skillet, preferably one with ridges to make attractive charred lines on the vegetables, and cook them briefly in batches, taking care not to overcook. Sprinkle with sea salt and rosemary before serving.

Preparation Time: 35 minutes.
Cooking Time: 20 minutes.

Variations
Other vegetables, such as wedges of fennel, small onions and cherry tomatoes can be cooked in this way.

Serve with Spicy Potato & Corn Cakes (page 56). The vegetables are also delicious mixed with pasta, sprinkled with cheese and accompanied by chunks of granary bread.

Eggplant Parmigiana

Serves 4

2 eggplants, sliced in $\frac{1}{2}$-inch rounds
Salt and pepper
5 tablespoons olive oil
$2\frac{1}{2}$ cups Tomato Sauce (page 36)
2 tablespoons fresh basil, finely chopped
2 cups Mozzarella cheese, grated
$\frac{1}{2}$ cup Parmesan cheese, grated

• Place the sliced eggplants on a plastic tray or dish, sprinkle with salt and allow to stand for 30 minutes.
• Preheat the oven to 350°F.
• Rinse the salt from the eggplants and dry on kitchen paper. Arrange the slices on a baking sheet and brush with olive oil. Cook in the oven for about 10 minutes, then remove. Turn the slices over and continue cooking for 15 minutes.
• Make the tomato sauce while the eggplants

are cooking.

- Place some tomato sauce on the bottom of a large oiled ovenproof dish. Arrange a layer of eggplants on top. Sprinkle with one-third of the Mozzarella, basil and Parmesan. Make three layers in this way, using slightly more cheese on the top layer.
- Bake in the oven for about 25-30 minutes until golden brown and bubbling. Allow to stand for 10 minutes before serving.

Preparation Time: 30 minutes.
Cooking Time: 1 hour.

Ratatouille

Serves 4-6
2 medium-sized eggplants
1 pound zucchini, 6 tablespoons oil
2 onions, sliced, 2-3 cloves garlic, crushed
6 tomatoes, skinned (preferably plum)
2 sweet peppers, deseeded
1 tablespoon chopped coriander
Salt and pepper, 1 teaspoon sugar (optional)
1 tablespoon chopped basil or parsley

- Slice the unpeeled eggplants and zucchini, sprinkle with salt and arrange on a plastic tray or in a colander. Leave to stand for at least 30 minutes. Rinse off the salt and dry with kitchen paper.
- Heat the oil in a deep frying pan or saucepan and cook the onions and garlic over a medium to low heat until transparent but not brown.
- Chop the tomatoes roughly and cut the peppers into strips.
- When the onions are soft, add the eggplants and allow to cook for 4 minutes. Add the peppers, cover with a lid and allow to simmer gently for about 15 minutes.
- Sprinkle with coriander and add the tomatoes and zucchini with salt, pepper and sugar if the tomatoes are not fully ripe. Simmer for about 45 minutes without a lid until the vegetables are soft but still retain some shape. Sprinkle with basil or parsley before serving hot or cold.

Preparation Time: 30 minutes.
Cooking Time: 1¼ hours.

Variation
Half this amount can be topped with slices of Brie cheese and lightly browned under the broiler. Serve hot, accompanied by wholewheat or French bread. Chill the remainder for serving cold as a starter.

Stuffed Eggplant

Serves 4
2 large eggplants
2 tablespoons oil
1 medium onion, finely diced
2 cloves garlic, crushed
1 cup mushrooms, diced
1 tablespoon mixed nuts
2 tablespoons white wine
1 tablespoon chopped parsley
1 cup cooked rice
1¼ cups Basic White Sauce (page 34)
½ cup grated cheese

- Cut the eggplants in half lengthways. With a sharp knife or grapefruit knife, remove the flesh to within ½ inch of the shells so that they remain intact. Cut the removed flesh into slices and sprinkle with salt. Leave for at least 20 minutes.
- Preheat the oven to 400°F. Oil a baking sheet or ovenproof dish.
- Heat the oil in a pan and cook the onion and garlic for about 4 minutes. Add the diced mushrooms.
- Rinse the eggplant flesh and dry on kitchen paper. Cut into small dice and add to the pan. Cook for 5 minutes. Add the white wine, nuts and rice and mix well with the chopped parsley.
- Spoon the mixture into the eggplant shells, dividing the white sauce among them and spread over the top. Sprinkle with grated cheese. Arrange on the oiled sheet or dish.
- Bake in the oven for 25-30 minutes or until golden brown.

Preparation Time: 30 minutes.
Cooking Time: 40 minutes.

Variation
Corn and Lemon Stuffing
Mix 8 ounces corn niblets with the juice and rind of 1 lemon.

Add to this the eggplant flesh, omitting the mushrooms and rice. Stuff and cook the eggplants as in previous recipe.

Ratatouille with grilled Brie

Mediterranean Stuffed Vegetables

Serves 4-8

2 large eggplants, halved lengthways
1 sweet green and 1 sweet yellow pepper,
halved lengthways
4 medium zucchini, halved lengthways
4 large ripe tomatoes

For the filling

3 tablespoons olive oil
1 large onion, finely chopped
2 cloves garlic, crushed
1 cup red lentils
1 sweet red pepper, deseeded
4 strips sun-dried tomatoes
Rind and juice of 1 lemon
1 teaspoon cinnamon, 1 teaspoon allspice
$\frac{1}{2}$ cup pine nuts, $\frac{1}{2}$ cup raisins
$\frac{1}{2}$ teaspoon cayenne pepper
Salt and pepper

For the topping

Lemon rind, 3 tablespoons chopped parsley
2 scallions, finely chopped
1 cup pine nuts, chopped
1 tablespoon olive oil

• Prepare the vegetables first. Scoop out the flesh of the eggplants with a sharp knife, leaving enough behind to keep the shell firm. Slice the eggplant flesh and put in a colander, sprinkled with salt.

• Deseed the peppers and blanch in boiling water for 2 minutes. Remove and drain well. Remove the zucchini flesh and cut into dice. Cut the stem tops from the tomatoes and carefully scoop out the flesh iinto a bowl.

• Heat the oil in a large saucepan and gently cook the onions, garlic and chopped red pepper for 4 minutes. Add the lentils and stir well. Pour in $1\frac{1}{4}$ cups stock or water. Cook covered for 10 minutes on a gentle heat, stirring from time to time.

• Preheat the oven to 400°F. Brush over a roasting tin with oil.

• Rinse the eggplant flesh and dry on kitchen paper, cut into small dice and add to the saucepan with the zucchini flesh, the inside of the tomatoes, lemon juice, spices, pine nuts and raisins and continue cooking for 10 minutes. Season with cayenne, salt and pepper.

• Fill all the vegetables with the lentil stuffing. Arrange the eggplants and peppers on the roasting tin, cover with aluminum foil and bake for 25 minutes.

• Meanwhile, prepare the topping by mixing the ingredients in a bowl. The mixture can also be prepared in a blender or food processor.

• Add the tomatoes and zucchini to the roasting tin, cover with the foil and cook for a further 20 minutes.

• To serve hot, remove the foil, sprinkle the topping on the vegetables, drizzle with olive oil and return to the oven for 5 minutes.

• To serve cold, add the topping and drizzle with olive oil. Serve with warmed French bread or olive ciabatta.

Preparation Time: 30 minutes.
Cooking Time: 1 hour.

This dish sounds complicated but is in fact simple as it uses the inside flesh of all the vegetables to make the filling. It is an excellent buffet dish. Long-grain brown or white rice can be used in place of lentils.

Oriental Stir Fry

Serves 4

4 tablespoons sunflower oil
2 garlic cloves, crushed
1 tablespoon fresh ginger, grated
2 zucchini, cut into slices
2 scallions, 8 ounces baby corn cobs
4 ounces snow peas, strips water chestnut
12 small broccoli florets
Pepper, soy sauce
2 tablespoons lemon juice
Thin strips of lemon peel
Sprigs of thyme and basil leaves

• Heat the oil in a wok or large skillet and add the garlic. Toss in the oil for 2 minutes over a medium heat and add the zucchini. Stir well, and move round in the wok with chop sticks or a spatula.

• Add the ginger to the vegetables, turning well. After 2 or 3 minutes, add the baby corn, scallions, water chestnut and snow peas and stir for a further 3 minutes before

Oriental Stir-Fry

adding the broccoli.

Cook until the vegetables are crisp or to your own taste. Season with pepper, soy sauce and lemon juice and garnish with the sprigs of fresh thyme, basil leaves and fine strips of lemon peel.

• Mix well before serving piping hot with a dish of rice or noodles.

Preparation Time: 20 minutes.
Cooking Time: Approx. 10-15 minutes.

Variation

Medley Stir-Fry

Any favorite vegetables can be stir-fried. Begin stir-frying the vegetables which take longest to cook such as carrots, celery, small turnips, celeriac, fennel, green beans, asparagus, whole scallions, cauliflower and broccoli florets and sugar snap peas. Follow these with fresh mushrooms, Chinese dried mushrooms (pre-soaked), baby corn, thin stick beans, bean sprouts and finally add

delicate vegetables such as Chinese cabbage, baby spinach, shredded lettuce and chopped scallions. Fruits such as sliced apples and sultanas can also be added, as can nuts.

Cabbage has a strong flavor and is often better stir-fried separately with apples and onions. Red and green cabbage together make an excellent stir-fry.

Medley Stir-Fry

Vegetable Chili

Serves 4

1 eggplant, sliced
4 zucchini, sliced, 2 large onions, chopped
2 garlic cloves, crushed
2 tablespoons oil, 1/4 cup butter or margarine
1 1/4 cups stock (page 12), salt and pepper
1 tablespoon cornstarch
16-ounce can crushed tomatoes
2 mild chilies, deseeded, or 1 hot chili
1/2-1 teaspoon chili powder
1 cup mushrooms, sliced if large
16-ounce can red kidney beans
2 tablespoons chopped coriander

- Stand the eggplant and zucchini slices in trays or colanders and leave to rest for 30 minutes, sprinkled with salt.
- Heat the oil and butter or margarine in a flameproof casserole or thick-bottomed saucepan and gently cook the onions and garlic over a low heat for about 5 minutes, stirring the vegetables together.
- Add the stock and simmer gently for 10 minutes. Make up the cornstarch with 2-3 tablespoons tomato juice from the can. Add a little seasoning and then tip in the can of tomatoes with the juice and the cornstarch mixture. Stir until the cornstarch starts to thicken the mixture.
- Rinse the zucchini and eggplant, dry on kitchen paper and cut the eggplant slices into small dice. Add to the pan.
- Dice the chilies finely and add with the chili powder (add a small amount at a time if you are unsure of their strength). Simmer the mixture for 15 minutes.
- Add the mushrooms, sliced if large, whole if small button mushrooms. Cook for another 10 minutes. Taste and add more chili powder, if necessary.
- Add the drained kidney beans, mixing well with a wooden spoon. Simmer for another 10 minutes.

• Sprinkle with plenty of chopped coriander and grated cheese and serve with baked potatoes, rice, pasta or tortillas.

Preparation Time: 20 minutes.
Cooking Time: 45 minutes.

Vegetable Chili

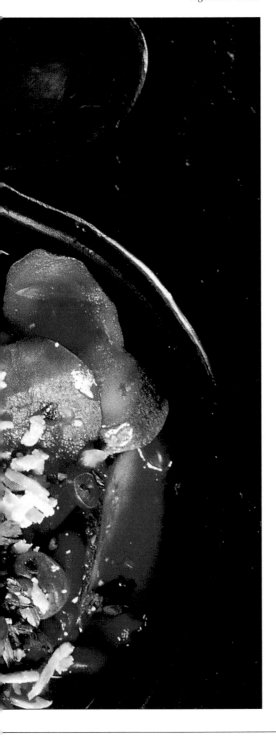

Mushroom Enchiladas

Serves 4
For the tomato sauce
2 tablespoons oil
1 onion, diced by hand or in food processor
1 carrot, diced by hand or in food processor
1-2 cloves garlic
16-ounce can crushed tomatoes
Salt and pepper
1/2 teaspoon oregano
1 tablespoon tomato paste
4 tablespoons white wine
For the mushroom sauce
1/4 cup butter
1 1/2 cups mushrooms, sliced
1 1/4 cups Béchamel Sauce (page 35)
1/2 teaspoon paprika
1 cup coarsely grated cheese
2/3 cup light cream
8 soft tortillas (enchiladas)(page 91)

• For a quick tomato sauce, prepare the onion, garlic and carrot in a food processor or chop roughly. Heat the oil and cook the vegetables for about 5 minutes in a saucepan over a low heat.
• Add all the other ingredients and simmer over a medium heat for 20 minutes. Sieve or put through the food processor or blender.
• Heat the butter and add the sliced mushrooms. Cook over a low heat for about 5 minutes.
• Make up the Béchamel sauce and add the cooked mushrooms. Mix well and season with paprika.
• Paint or spread the tortillas with some of the tomato sauce. Heat a pan, brushed over with oil, and fry them over a high heat for about 20 seconds each side.
• Preheat the oven to 350°F.
• Fill each tortilla with the mushroom mixture. Place them seam sides down on an oiled ovenproof baking dish. Pour over the remaining tomato sauce. Drizzle the tortillas with cream and sprinkle with cheese. Bake in the oven for 20 minutes. These tortillas resemble cannelloni when cooked.

Preparation time: 30 minutes.
Cooking Time: 30 minutes.

Tortillas with Chili

Serves 4
1/2 quantity Vegetable Chili (opposite page)
For the avocado topping
1 ripe avocado
1 tablespoon lemon juice
1/2 teaspoon chili sauce
2 tablespoons light sour cream
Salt and pepper
4 tablespoons oil
8 soft tortillas (page 91)

• Heat the Vegetable Chili and keep warm.
• Cut the avocado in two and scrape out the flesh into a bowl. Mash with the lemon juice, seasonings and cream.
• Heat the oil in a large frying pan. Drop in each tortilla, allowing 20 seconds on each side for them to heat through. Drain on kitchen paper and arrange in aluminum foil in a low oven to keep warm until all the tortillas are ready.
• Spread the hot chili onto each tortilla, add a spoonful of the avocado mixture, roll it up and eat immediately. Serve with a green salad with scallions, slices of tomato and heated refried beans.

Preparation Time: 50 minutes.
Cooking Time: 45 minutes.

Heating tortillas
To heat bought or home-made soft tortillas in the microwave oven, place not more than 8 wrapped together in a paper napkin or kitchen paper. Heat through for 30 seconds and use immediately.

Crisp corn tortillas can be heated in the oven for 10 minutes, filled with Vegetable Chili (opposite) and served topped with sour cream and a mixed salad.

Curry Powder

Regular users of commercial curry powder may like to make the real thing for themselves as it is infinitely more aromatic.

4 ounces ground turmeric
4 ounces coriander seeds
4 ounces cumin seeds
$\frac{1}{2}$ cup powdered ginger
2 peppercorns
1 tablespoon cardamom pods
1 tablespoon fennel seeds
1 tablespoon dried chilies
1 tablespoon mace
1 tablespoon whole cloves
2 teaspoons mustard seeds
2 teaspoons poppy seeds

- Blend the spices together in a small blender or in a pestle and mortar, which will take much longer. Make only small quantities of curry powder at a time as the spices, being highly volatile, quickly become stale.
- Store in an air-tight jar or box. More chili will make the mixture hotter.

Variation
Fenugreek and garlic powder can also be used in curry powders and there are many other excellent spices available at specialist and oriental stores.

Cauliflower & Tomato Curry

Serves 4
4 tablespoons oil
1 large onion, diced
1-2 garlic cloves, crushed
1 tablespoon curry powder
(see above)
4 stalks celery, finely diced
8 ounces peeled tomatoes, quartered
Salt and pepper
1 tablespoon lemon juice
1 small cauliflower,
cut into florets
1 tablespoon wholewheat flour
$3\frac{3}{4}$ cups stock (page 12)
For the garnish
1 large onion, cut into rings
2 tablespoons oil

Cauliflower & Tomato Curry

- Heat the oil in a large saucepan. Add the onion and garlic and allow to cook on a low heat for about 5 minutes.
- Sprinkle in the curry powder and raise the heat for 2 minutes, stirring the powder and onions to avoid sticking. Add the celery. Cook, stirring with a spatula, for about 2 minutes. Season well.
- Sprinkle with lemon juice, then the flour and mix well. Add the stock and stir over a medium heat until the mixture comes to the boil. Cover and simmer for 20 minutes, then add the cauliflower and cook until all the vegetables are tender. Add the tomatoes and serve as soon as they are cooked, about 5 minutes. Garnish with the onion rings which have been fried to a golden brown.

Preparation Time: 20 minutes.
Cooking Time: 45 minutes.

Variations
Any combination of vegetables can be used for added variety.

Eggplants, mushrooms, peppers, chilies, beans, sweet potatoes, are all suitable. Time recipe carefully since some vegetables take longer to cook than others. So add after cooking root vegetables and test from time to time how they are progressing.

Squash and Zucchini Curry
Cut the squash and zucchini into dice, add to the pan with the onion, garlic and curry powder. Omit the potato if you wish. Garnish the curry with toasted almonds.

Vegetable Curry

Serves 4

4 tablespoons oil, 1 large onion, diced
1-2 garlic cloves, crushed
2 carrots, diced, 2 stalks celery, sliced
1 tablespoon medium curry powder
1 tablespoon flour
1 medium can chopped tomatoes
1 cup stock (page 12)
salt and pepper
1 sweet red and 1 sweet yellow pepper,
deseeded
1 tablespoon sultanas
$1/4$ cup dried apricots, chopped
1 pound textured vegetable protein
1 pound broccoli spears

- Heat the oil in a saucepan and cook the onions and garlic over a low heat for 5 minutes. Add the carrots and celery and continue cooking for 2 minutes.
- Increase the heat to medium and sprinkle the curry powder on the vegetables. Cook for at least 1 minute, then mix in the flour. Add the tomatoes and the stock and mix well. Season with salt and pepper and allow to simmer gently.
- Dice the peppers and blanch in boiling water for 4 minutes, drain and add to the curry. Simmer for 10 minutes.
- Add the dried fruit and the textured vegetable protein and simmer gently for 15 minutes. Taste for flavor, then add the broccoli spears. Cook until the broccoli is tender. A little chili powder will make the curry hotter and a few drops of lemon or lime juice will enhance the flavor. Serve with herbed or fried rice, naan bread and mango chutney.

Preparation Time: 15 minutes.
Cooking Time: 40 minutes.

Textured vegetable proteins are now widely available. Experiment with small quantities until you find one to your liking.

Vegetable Curry

Smoked Tofu Kebabs

Serves 4

8 ounces smoked tofu
2 green peppers, deseeded
24 button mushrooms
2 limes
2 tablespoons olive oil
1 tablespoon chili sauce

- Cut the tofu into even-sized cubes and place in a bowl.
- Cut the green peppers into squares and blanch in boiling water for 1 minute. Drain well and add to the tofu with the washed and dried mushrooms.
- Squeeze the juice of 1 lime into the bowl with the tofu and vegetables and mix with the oil and chili sauce. Allow to stand for 30 minutes.
- Arrange tofu, mushrooms and green pepper alternately on metal skewers. Brush over with the marinade and cook on a barbecue or under a very hot broiler. Turn after 3 minutes, cook for 8-10 minutes in all. Serve with plain couscous or rice and vegetables.

Preparation Time: 10 minutes plus 30 minutes standing.
Cooking Time: 10 minutes.

Variation
Fried Tofu with Leeks and Sweet Red Peppers

- Marinate a pack of tofu cut into squares with diced sweet red pepper in place of the green. Allow to stand for 30 minutes at least.
- Beat up an egg on a plate and prepare another flat plate with dried breadcrumbs. Dip the squares of tofu in egg and then into crumbs. Strain the red pepper but retain the marinade.

Wash and dry 2 leeks and cut into slices.
- Heat a frying pan with ¹/₂ inch oil in the bottom, fry the cubes of tofu until crisp on both sides, drain on kitchen paper and keep warm.
- Strain a little oil into a clean pan and add 2 tablespoons butter. When the fat is hot add the peppers and the leeks and toss about for 2 minutes in the fat. Turn the heat down and allow the vegetables to cook for about 6-7 minutes. Mix with the fried tofu and sprinkle with chopped parsley. Serve with a potato or noodle dish.

Vegetable Pie Topped with Potato

Serves 4
2¹/₄ pounds peeled potatoes
2 carrots, sliced
1 tablespoon oil
2 cloves garlic, crushed
2 leeks, sliced
2 zucchini, sliced
16-ounce can plum tomatoes with juice
16-ounce can beans
2 tablespoons butter or margarine
1 egg (optional)
3 tablespoons milk or cream
4 tablespoons grated cheese

- Prepare the potatoes by cooking until soft. Mash or rice to remove all the lumps and leave in a bowl. Prepare the carrots and blanch in boiling water for 3 minutes, drain in a colander.
- Heat the oil and add the garlic, leeks and drained carrots. Cook over a low heat for 3 minutes. Add the zucchini and canned tomatoes. Arrange in a buttered ovenproof dish.
- Cover the vegetables with the beans. Preheat the oven to 350°F.
- Mix the potatoes with egg and cream as desired. Pipe or fork on top of the vegetables. Sprinkle with grated cheese. Cook in the oven for 25 minutes until golden brown.

Preparation Time: 20 minutes.
Cooking Time: 1 hour.

Variations
Eggplants, onions, kidney beans, baked beans, fresh tomatoes, broccoli, green beans and French beans can all be used.

For a crispy topping, use breadcrumbs, crushed cornflakes or chopped peanuts mixed with the cheese to top the potatoes.

Smoked Tofu Kebabs accompanied by couscous and root and green vegetables

Couscous

This is a vegetarian adaptation of a North African dish. If a traditional *cous-cousier* is not available, use a sieve or fine strainer fitted over a thick-bottomed saucepan.

Serves 4
2 tablespoons oil
1 teaspoon paprika
2 teaspoons yellow mustard seeds
1 onion, finely chopped
3 cloves of garlic, crushed
1 sweet red, 1 green, 1 yellow pepper, deseeded and diced
1 pound plum or ripe tomatoes, skinned and chopped
12 ounces zucchini, sliced
2 medium-sized potatoes, boiled for 5 minutes, peeled and diced
6 ounces okra, topped and diced
¹/₃ cup raisins
2¹/₂ cups stock (page 12)
8 ounces couscous, soaked in a bowl for 10 minutes
Salt and pepper

- Heat the oil in a large saucepan, add all the spices and fry for about 2 minutes. Add the onion and garlic and fry for 1 minute, turning in the spices. Add all the remaining vegetables and the raisins.
- Put the vegetables in the *cous-cousier* or leave in the saucepan and arrange a muslin-lined sieve or strainer to fit over the pan with the drained couscous in the top. Pour the stock over the vegetables and allow to steam gently for 25 minutes, uncovered, making sure that the couscous does not touch the vegetable stew.
- When the vegetables are tender and the couscous light and fluffy, turn the couscous onto a heated serving plate and serve with the vegetable stew. For extra flavor, texture and color, very thin strips of raw carrot and lemon rind can be added to the couscous while cooking.

Preparation Time: 20 minutes.
Cooking Time: 30 minutes.

Eastern Tofu with Snow Peas

Serves 4

8 ounces smoked tofu
1 piece of preserved ginger,
cut into thin slices
4 tablespoons sweet and sour sauce
1 teaspoon chili sauce, 4 tablespoons oil
1/2 inch fresh ginger, grated
12 ounces snow peas,
topped and tailed
1 tablespoon sesame seeds
1 tablespoon soy sauce

• Cut the tofu into squares and put in a bowl with the preserved ginger, sweet and sour sauce, and chili sauce. Stir well and leave to marinade for at least 1 hour. Drain through a sieve, retaining the liquid and ginger.

• Heat the oil in a wok or frying pan, add the tofu and fry until golden on each side. Add the grated ginger with the snow peas and stir-fry all together for 3-4 minutes. Add the slices of preserved ginger, heat briefly, and serve sprinkled with the sesame seeds.

• Add a little soy sauce to the marinade with 2 tablespoons water, heat, and serve in a bowl separately.

Preparation Time: 5 minutes plus 1 hour marinating.
Cooking Time: 10 minutes.

Eastern Tofu with Snow Peas

Smoked Tofu Strips

Serves 4

8 ounces smoked tofu
2 tablespoons all-purpose flour
Salt and pepper
1 egg, beaten
1 1/2 tablespoons fresh breadcrumbs
Oil for frying

• Cut the tofu into thin strips about 2 1/2 inches long.

• Add 1 tablespoon water to the egg and mix well. Dip the strips into the flour seasoned with salt and pepper. Dip into the egg and finally into the breadcrumbs.

• Heat the oil in a deep pan and wait until a bread square, when dropped in, rises

immediately to the surface. Fry the strips in batches, keeping each batch warm. Serve with spicy dips as a starter or with a vegetable and potato dish as a main course.

Preparation Time: 10 minutes.
Cooking Time: 12-14 minutes.

Spinach & Potato Gratin

Serves 4

2¹/₂ pounds peeled potatoes, 1 egg, beaten
2 tablespoons milk or cream
Knob of butter, salt and pepper
2¹/₂ pounds fresh spinach, washed
2 tablespoons oil, 1 large onion, diced
1 clove garlic, crushed, ³/₄ cup ricotta cheese

¹/₂ cup raisins
¹/₄ teaspoon freshly grated nutmeg
¹/₂ pint Béchamel Sauce (page 35)
2 tablespoons light sour cream
1-2 tablespoons fresh breadcrumbs

• Boil the potatoes until soft, drain well and rice or sieve or mash well. Mix in the egg, milk, butter, nutmeg and cream with a wooden spoon until smooth. Put the spinach in 4 tablespoons boiling water and cook for 3 minutes, drain well. Make the sauce.

• Heat the oil and over a low heat cook the onion and garlic without browning for about 4 minutes, then add the raisins. Cook for a further 3 minutes, turning the mixture from time to time.

• Preheat the oven to 400°F.

• Spread half the ricotta cheese on the bottom of an ovenproof dish. Chop the spinach and mix with the onions, garlic and raisins. Spread the mixture over the ricotta in the dish and pour the sauce over the spinach.

• Pipe or fork the potatoes round the edges and spread the cream over the sauce. Sprinkle with the remaining ricotta and the breadcrumbs. Bake in the oven for 20 minutes or until golden brown.

Preparation Time: 35 minutes.
Cooking Time: 35 minutes.

Spinach & Potato Gratin

Fried Polenta with Herbs & Mushrooms

Serves 4-6

$1/4$ cup vegetable oil, 1 onion, finely diced
2 cups mushrooms, chopped
1 tablespoon chopped fresh tarragon
Salt, $1/2$ teaspoon paprika
Polenta (see previous recipe)
Cornmeal for coating, vegetable oil for frying
2 sprigs rosemary

- Heat the oil in a frying pan, add the onion and allow to cook for 3-4 minutes on a low heat. Add the mushrooms to the pan and stir to mix well. Stir salt, paprika and tarragon into the mushroom mixture. Remove from the heat after 5 minutes.
- Cook the polenta as previously instructed but add the mushroom mixture half way through the cooking time. Finish cooking and allow to cool before slicing.
- Heat the oil for frying with the rosemary. Dip the polenta slices in cornmeal or flour and fry until golden. Serve with a sauce.

Preparation time: 20 minutes plus 1 hour cooling time.
Cooking Time: 45 minutes to prepare polenta, 15 minutes to fry.

Polenta with Spicy Sauce

Serves 4

8 ounces yellow cornmeal
1 teaspoon salt, $1/4$ cup butter
For the sauce
2 tablespoons olive oil
1 large onion, finely chopped
2 cloves garlic, crushed
$1/2$ teaspoon chili powder
2 sweet red peppers, deseeded and diced
16-ounce can plum tomatoes
1 tablespoon tomato paste
Salt and pepper, chopped sage
For the coating
1 egg, beaten
Cornmeal for coating
Oil for deep frying
For sprinkling
$1/2$ cup cheese (optional)

- Pour 1 quart water into a large saucepan and bring to the boil. Sprinkle on the cornmeal gradually, stirring constantly.
- Add the salt and butter and continue

Polenta and Spicy Sauce

cooking over a low heat in a covered saucepan for 20 minutes. Stir every few minutes. The mixture should be thick and creamy when cooked.
- Oil a wide shallow dish and pour in the polenta to cool; it should be about $1/2$ inch thick.
- To make the sauce, heat the oil in a frying pan and cook the onion and garlic for about 4 minutes. Add the chili and red peppers and cook for another 3 minutes. Stir in the tomatoes and the paste and simmer for 20 minutes until the sauce thickens. Season with salt and pepper and chopped sage.
- Cut the polenta into squares when cool. Dip in beaten egg and cornmeal. Heat the oil and deep fry. Drain on kitchen paper. Serve on a plate, covered with sauce and cheese or serve with a vegetable bake or casserole.

Preparation Time: 15 minutes plus 1 hour cooling time.
Cooking Time: 45 minutes.

Spicy Potato & Corn Cakes

Serves 4

2 potatoes, peeled
1 zucchini
2 tablespoons canned corn kernels, drained
$1/2$ cup wholewheat flour
1 beaten egg
1 scallion, finely chopped
1 tablespoon chopped parsley or coriander
$1/2$ teaspoon mild curry powder or paste
Salt and pepper
Oil for frying

- Grate the potatoes and zucchini in a food processor or by hand. Place in a sieve and squeeze out the water. Pat dry with kitchen paper and put into a bowl.
- Add the corn, flour, egg, onion, parsley and

curry powder or paste. Season with salt and pepper. Mix well and form into cakes.

• Heat the oil in a pan and drop in the potato cakes. Fry for 4 -5 minutes each side. Keep warm until all the cakes are fried.

Preparation Time: 15 minutes.
Cooking Time: 24 minutes.

Potato & Leek Gratin

Serves 4

6 medium-sized potatoes,
washed but unpeeled
Salt and pepper
1 tablespoon oil
2 tablespoons butter
1 large onion, thinly sliced
2 cloves garlic, crushed
2 leeks, washed and thinly sliced
1 1/4 cups Béchamel Sauce (page 35) or milk
2-3 tablespoons sour cream
1/2 cup strong cheese, grated
2 tablespoons wholewheat breadcrumbs

• This recipe can be prepared in a few minutes using a food processor. Preheat the oven to 350°F.

• Place the potatoes in cold water with a little salt. Bring to the boil and cook for 5 minutes. Drain and cool slightly.

• Heat the oil and butter in a frying pan, add the sliced onion and garlic and cook over a low heat for about 4 minutes, then add the sliced leeks and cook for a further 4 minutes.

• Peel the potatoes and slice thinly and evenly. Using an ovenproof dish about 2 1/2 inches deep, put one-third of the onion mixture on the bottom and cover with slices of potato. Use one-third of the sauce or boiling milk and pour over. Season and sprinkle with a little cheese.

• Continue in this way to form three layers, keeping some sauce (if using) for the top. Season, spread on the cream and finish with cheese and breadcrumbs. Bake in the oven for 1 hour but test the potatoes at 45 minutes; or, if preferred, cook at a lower temperature with a longer cooking time if this is more convenient.

Preparation Time: 20 minutes.
Cooking Time: 1 hour.

Spicy Potato & Corn Cakes

Variations
Other vegetables make excellent gratins and can be added to suit individual taste. Chopped herbs such as parsley, chervil and chives can also be included.

Mushroom Gratin
Substitute 2 cups sliced mushrooms for the leeks.

Mixed Gratin
Eggplants, peppers and zucchini are also delicious in a gratin. Omit the potatoes and use celeriac (celery root) and carrots. Jerusalem artichokes are excellent mixed with potatoes.

Any crumbly cheese can be used and it is a good way of using up left-over scraps.

Barley & Tomatoes in Sour Cream Sauce

Serves 4

1 tablespoon oil, 1 cup pearl barley
1 1/4 pounds tomatoes, skinned
1/4 cup black olives, pitted and chopped

2 cups mushrooms, sliced
1 teaspoon dill (fresh if possible)
1 cup sour cream, 1 cup grated cheese
Salt and pepper

• Heat the oil in a large pan over a moderate heat and fry the barley for 3 minutes, stirring all the time. Add enough boiling water to cover the barley by 2 inches. Cover the pan and simmer for 45-60 minutes until tender. Drain in a sieve.

• Preheat the oven to 375°F.

• Chop half the tomatoes roughly and mix with the barley, olives, mushrooms, dill, sour cream and half the cheese. Season well with salt and pepper and turn into an ovenproof dish.

• Slice the remaining tomatoes and arrange them in a layer on the top. Sprinkle over the rest of the cheese and bake for 15 minutes or until golden brown.

Preparation Time: 15 minutes.
Cooking Time: 1 1/4 hours.

Stuffed Leaves

Large, firm lettuce, as well as cabbage leaves, can be filled with a variety of stuffings. The rice and pine nut stuffing for Dolmades on page 26 is an alternative filling.

Serves 4

For the stuffing

1 tablespoon olive oil, 1 onion, finely diced
1 carrot, grated, rind and juice of 1 lemon,
1½ cups fresh breadcrumbs
1 cup walnuts or shelled chestnuts, chopped
2 ounces dried no-soak apricots, chopped
2 tablespoons chopped parsley, 1 egg
8 large iceberg lettuce leaves
2 pounds spinach, washed and destalked
2 tablespoons flaked almonds
Salt and pepper

- To make the stuffing, heat the oil in a frying pan over a low heat and cook the onion gently until it becomes transparent. Add the

carrot after about 4 minutes and cook for a further 2 minutes.

- Tip the mixture into a bowl, add the lemon, breadcrumbs, nuts, apricots and parsley. Stir well and then mix to a firm consistency with the egg.
- Bring a large pan of salted water to the boil and put in the leaves for 1 minute to blanch. Drain well.
- Preheat the oven to 350°F.
- Place each leaf on a board and place a portion of stuffing on each, rolling them up into cigar shapes.
- Cook the spinach in very little water for 5 minutes, drain very well and chop. Season well. Serve the stuffed leaves on a bed of the spinach to which the flaked almonds have been added.

Preparation Time: 20 minutes.
Cooking Time: 50 minutes.

Savory Barley Casserole

Serves 4-6

1 teaspoon butter, 1 cup pot barley
3 cups vegetable stock (page 12)
2 onions, finely chopped
1 sweet green and 1 red pepper, deseeded and cut into small squares
2 large tomatoes, cut into quarters
1 tablespoon fresh oregano, salt and pepper
2 cups grated cheese

- Preheat the oven to 350°F. Butter an ovenproof dish. Mix the barley, stock, onions, peppers, tomatoes and oregano in the dish and season well. Cover and cook in the oven for 45 minutes.
- Remove lid and sprinkle with the cheese. Return to the oven uncovered for 25-30 minutes until most of the liquid is absorbed.

Preparation Time: 10 minutes.
Cooking Time: 75 minutes.

Potato Kebabs

Serves 4

1 large eggplant, sliced in half lengthways
12 small new potatoes, scrubbed
8 shallots or pickling onions
8 button mushrooms
2 sweet green peppers, deseeded
8 bay leaves
For the herb oil
4 tablespoons olive oil
2 sprigs parsley
1 teaspoon oregano
1 bay leaf

• Put the oil, parsley, oregano and bay leaf into a screw-top jar and shake vigorously.
• Sprinkle the eggplant slices with salt and stand on a plastic tray for 30 minutes. Wash and dry with a paper towel and cut the slice into 4 pieces.
• Put the potatoes in boiling salted water and cook for 8 minutes. Drain into a colander. Drop the onions into the water for the last 2 minutes and drain with the potatoes.

• Cut the peppers into squares. Thread the skewers with pepper, onion, eggplant, mushroom, potato, interspersed with bay leaves, and begin again with the pepper until the skewer is full. Lay the kebabs on a flat dish and paint with the herb oil.
• Heat the broiler to high and place the dish with the kebabs underneath. Cook on each side for 3 minutes, then turn the heat down to medium and allow the kebabs to cook for another 3-4 minutes, turning to make sure all sides of the vegetables are cooked.

Preparation: 15 minutes.
Cooking Time: 20 minutes.

Variation
Other vegetables can be added or substituted for the ones in the recipe, such as whole cherry tomatoes or chunks of zucchini.

OPPOSITE: *Stuffed Leaves*
BELOW: *Potato Kebabs*

Corn on the Cob

Serves 4

4 corncobs, husks removed
1/4 cup butter
1 tablespoon black or green olives, pitted and sliced
1 teaspoon capers
2 scallions, chopped
1/2 sweet red pepper, deseeded and cut into small dice
1/2 cup mushrooms, washed and chopped
Salt and pepper

• Cook the corncobs in boiling water for 10 minutes until tender.
• Melt the butter in a small pan and add the remaining ingredients. Heat through for about 2 minutes.
• Drain the corn and serve with the savory butter spooned on top.

Variation
The corncobs can be cooked in their husks on the barbecue or wrapped in aluminum foil and baked in the oven.

for 4 potatoes). They can then be crisped up by putting under a broiler for a few minutes or placing in a hot oven for 10 minutes.

Preparation Time: 5 minutes.
Cooking Time: 1 hour.

To Fill Baked Potatoes

• Cut the potatoes in half lengthways and scoop out some of the insides into a bowl.
• Mix with whatever filling is being used. Fill the potatoes and return to the oven or microwave to reheat for a few minutes. Stuffed potatoes can be prepared in advance, stored in the refrigerator and heated through before serving.

Cheesy Baked Potatoes

The following recipes are for 4 baked potatoes, prepared as above
2 tablespoons butter or margarine
2-3 tablespoons milk, ¹/₂ cup grated cheese
¹/₂ teaspoon mustard, 2 tablespoons cream
Salt and pepper

• Cut the cooked potatoes in half. Scoop out their insides and mix with the milk and butter. Add ³/₄ of the cheese and the remaining ingredients, beating well with a wooden spoon. Season to taste.
• Stuff the filling back into the potato halves and sprinkle with the remaining cheese. Reheat for 10-15 minutes.

Baked Potatoes with Cottage Cheese & Walnuts

¹/₂ cup cottage cheese
1 tablespoon chopped parsley
Salt and pepper
¹/₂ cup walnuts, chopped

• Mix all the ingredients together with the insides of the potatoes. Stuff mixture back into the potato shells and reheat.

Variation
Finely slice a stick of celery and mix with 2 finely chopped scallions and the cottage cheese. Season with salt, pepper and a pinch of paprika.

Baked Potatoes

Serves 4
4 large even-sized potatoes, washed and scrubbed
¹/₄ cup butter or margarine

• Preheat the oven to 350°F.
• Prick the potatoes all over with a fork and make a cross on the top of the best side.
• Place on the oven shelf and bake for 1 hour or less if smaller potatoes are used.

Baked Potatoes with Ratatouille (page 45) and sour cream

• Remove from the oven and squeeze the top of the potato to open the cross out. Alternatively, the potatoes can be cut in half before filling.
• If serving plain, season and add a knob of butter to each half.
To save time, baked potatoes can be cooked in the microwave, but they will have soft skins. Allow 5 minutes for each potato (20 minutes

Baked Potatoes with Sour Cream & Chive Filling

1 cup sour cream
2 tablespoons chopped chives
1 tablespoon chopped coriander (optional)
Salt and pepper

• Mix all the ingredients with the insides of the potatoes and return to the shells.

Other Fillings

Vegetable Chili Filling

Use half the Vegetable Chili recipe (page 48) for 4 potatoes. Squeeze the cross at the top of the cooked potatoes and add a pat of butter. Serve the chili on top and around the potatoes.

Saucy Fillings

Use $1^1/4$ cups cheese sauce (page 34) and mix with 1 cup chopped, lightly-cooked mushrooms.

Alternatively, use 8 ounces corn in place of the mushrooms.

To fill with sauce, a little of the potato inside must be removed or squashed down.

Garlic Mushrooms with Yogurt

Fry 1 cup sliced button mushrooms in $^1/4$ cup butter or margarine with 1 crushed garlic clove. Mix 4 tablespoons natural yogurt with 2 tablespoons chopped fresh chives. Mash the inside of the potatoes down with a fork, add $^1/4$ mushroom mixture to each potato and top with yogurt.

Guacamole and Sour Cream

Make up the Guacamole (page 22). Remove some of the potato from their skins when cooked, mash and return with a topping of guacamole and sour cream.

Ratatouille and Sour Cream

(see picture opposite)
Use one-third of the recipe on page 45 but cut the vegetables into smaller dice.

Egg Nests

Serves 4
4 large baking potatoes, washed
$^1/2$ cup butter, melted
Salt and pepper
8 small eggs
1 cup grated cheese (optional)

• Bake the potatoes as directed (opposite). Remove from the oven and halve lengthways.
• Remove some of the potato from the shell. (Set aside for mashing.)
• Season the shells and break 1 egg into each. Season with salt and pepper.
• Top with butter and cheese, return the nests to the hot oven and cook until the egg whites are firm. Serve immediately.

Preparation Time: 10 minutes.
Cooking Time: $1^3/4$ hours.

Provençal Potatoes

Serves 4-6
2 pounds potatoes
Salt and pepper
2 large onions, chopped
1 pound ripe tomatoes, sliced
$1^1/2$ cups grated Swiss cheese
1 tablespoon fresh thyme leaves
$^2/3$ cup olive oil

• Wash the potatoes but do not peel. Place in a pan of cold salted water, bring to the boil and cook until tender but still firm. Drain and allow to cool.
• Peel the potatoes and cut into slices. Preheat the oven to 425°F.
• Brush an ovenproof dish with oil. Arrange layers of potato, tomato, onion and cheese. Sprinkle each layer with salt, pepper and thyme.
• Top with a layer of tomatoes sprinkled with cheese and thyme. Drizzle the olive oil over the top and bake until golden brown for about 20 minutes.

Preparation Time: 20 minutes.
Cooking Time: 40 minutes.

Spinach Soufflé Potatoes

Serves 4
4 large baking potatoes, washed
1 pound fresh or frozen spinach
$^1/2$ cup butter
Salt and pepper
4 tablespoons sour cream
Grated nutmeg
4 eggs

• Preheat the oven to 350°F and bake the potatoes as directed (opposite).
• Cook the fresh spinach for about 5 minutes in a small amount of boiling water. Drain well in a colander. Cook frozen spinach as directed on the package. If necessary, chop the spinach after cooking.
• Return the spinach to the hot pan to evaporate any residual water. Add $^1/4$ cup butter, season and mix well.
• Remove the tops from the potatoes and spoon the flesh out into a bowl, taking care not to damage the shells.
• Divide the spinach among the potatoes, spoon over the cream and sprinkle with nutmeg, salt and pepper. Arrange on a baking sheet.
• Separate the yolks and whites of the eggs into different bowls. Add the sieved or riced potato mixture to the egg yolks with salt and pepper and half the remaining butter.
• Whisk the egg whites until light and fluffy but not too stiff. Fold into the potato mixture until well incorporated and spoon into the potatoes. Bake for 20-25 minutes until golden and fluffy.

Preparation Time: 20 minutes.
Cooking Time: 2 hours including baking time for potatoes.

Variation
Sprinkle the tops of the potatoes with grated cheese and paprika pepper before baking in the oven. 2 tablespoons grated cheese can be added to the potato mixture.

Mixed Bean Cobbler

Serves 4

8 ounces navy beans, soaked
8 ounces lima beans, soaked
4 ounces kidney beans, soaked
1 large potato, peeled and diced
Bay leaf
Bouquet garni
3 tablespoons oil
2 medium onions, diced
2 garlic cloves, crushed
3 stalks celery, sliced
2 zucchini, halved and sliced
16-ounce can tomatoes
$2/3$ cup tomato purée
(sieved tomatoes)
$2/3$ cup red wine
2 cups stock (page 12)
For the cobbler
1 cup wholewheat flour
1 teaspoon salt
1 teaspoon baking powder
1 cup butter or margarine
$1/4$ teaspoon French mustard
1 teaspoon dried mixed herbs or
1 tablespoon chopped fresh parsley
1 tablespoon grated cheese (optional)
3-4 tablespoons cold water

- Soak the beans overnight. Briskly cook them next day in boiling water for at least 10 minutes. Rinse well and drain. Cook the diced potato in boiling salted water for 5 minutes and drain. Add the bay leaf and the bouquet garni.
- Preheat the oven to 350°F.
- Heat the oil and cook the onion and garlic in a large casserole for about 5 minutes, then add the celery and zucchini.
- Add the beans to the casserole and cook for 30 minutes in the oven. Remove from the oven and mix in the tomatoes, tomato purée and stock. Season well and add the herbs and wine. Bring to the boil and simmer for 10 minutes on top of the cooking stove.
- Return the casserole to the oven for about 45 minutes when the beans should be very nearly cooked. Increase the oven temperature to 400°F.
- Meanwhile, sift the flour and baking powder into a bowl with the herbs and seasoning. Rub in the butter or margarine until the mixture resembles fine breadcrumbs. Mix with the water to form a soft dough and turn out onto a floured board.
- Roll out evenly and cut into 2-inch rounds with a cutter. Brush with milk or beaten egg and arrange the scones on top of the vegetables. Return once more to the oven and cook for 20 minutes until the scones are cooked and golden brown. Sprinkle the center with chopped parsley.

Preparation time: 1 hour plus 8 hours soaking time for beans.
Cooking Time: $1\frac{1}{2}$ hours.

Mixed Bean Cobbler

Canned beans can be used for this recipe. After adding the beans, cook for 15 minutes and then for 20 minutes with the scone topping.

Crêpes

Crêpe batter must be smooth and no thicker than thin cream. A thick batter will not make thin crêpes.

Makes 12 crêpes
1 cup all-purpose flour
Pinch of salt
1 large egg, beaten
1¼ cups milk

- Sift the flour into a bowl with the salt. Make a well in the center of the flour and drop in the egg.
- Gradually add half the milk, stirring with a wooden spoon and allowing the flour to fall into the center of the bowl in a thin film onto the liquid.
- Using a whisk, beat in the remaining milk until the mixture is smooth.
- Allow to stand for 30 minutes to allow the starch grains to swell.
- Heat an omelet pan or small skillet and brush over with a small amount of oil (too much will make heavy crêpes).
- When the fat is hot, remove the pan from the heat and pour enough batter into the pan to cover the bottom in a thin layer. Swirl the batter round the pan to cover the base and then replace pan on the heat. Cook until little bubbles form all over the surface. Loosen the edges of the crêpe with a palette knife and turn it over.
- When golden on the underside, tip onto wax paper and put a layer of wax paper between each one. They can be kept warm in a low oven while cooking the remainder.
- Fill and serve as required.

Preparation Time: 10 minutes plus 30 minutes standing (this standing time is not strictly necessary if pressed for time).
Cooking Time: 15 minutes.

Variations
These crêpes can be served as a dessert, sprinkled with caster sugar and lemon juice. They are also ideal in savory dishes, stuffed with vegetables mixed with a sauce.

The batter can be used to make Yorkshire pudding in the oven. For this it is better to use 2 eggs in the basic batter mix.

It is best to keep a small pan specially reserved for omelets and crêpes as the mixture can stick in ordinary frying pans which have been used for frying other foods.

Vegetable Pudding with Onion Gravy

Serves 4
1 recipe Crêpes batter
1 tablespoon oil
1 cauliflower,
broken into florets
1 head broccoli,
broken into florets
For the onion gravy
1 large onion, finely chopped
2 tablespoons butter or margarine
2 tablespoons all-purpose flour
1¼ cups brown vegetable stock (page 12)
Salt and pepper
2 tablespoons red wine (optional)

- Make up the batter. Put the oil in a 2 inch deep ovenproof dish into the oven and preheat the oven to 450°F.
- Cook the cauliflower in boiling salted water for 5 minutes, then add the broccoli florets and cook for a further 5 minutes. Drain into a colander.
- Remove the dish from the oven and arrange the cauliflower and broccoli in alternate rows. Pour on the batter and return the tin to the oven as quickly as possible. Cook for 20-25 minutes until the batter is light and fluffy.
- Meanwhile, heat the butter or margarine in a saucepan and fry the onions over a medium heat until they are golden brown but do not allow them to burn. Sprinkle in the flour and allow it to brown, gradually whisking in the stock. Allow to simmer, whisking from time to time to prevent lumping. Cook gently for about 15 minutes for a rich gravy. Season well and add 2 tablespoons red wine which will greatly improve the flavor.
- Serve pudding and onion sauce separately.

Preparation Time: 30 minutes.
Cooking Time: 35 minutes.

Variation
Tomato or Sweet Pepper Sauce (pages 36 and 38) can be served in place of onion gravy.

Sweet Pepper Pancakes

Makes 12 small pancakes
1 small onion
1 sweet red pepper, deseeded and sliced
2 eggs, separated, $\frac{1}{4}$ cup ricotta cheese
1 cup all-purpose flour
$\frac{1}{4}$ teaspoon pepper
$\frac{1}{2}$ pint Tomato Sauce (page 36)
8 scallions

- Chop the onion in a blender or food processor for about 30 seconds, followed by the red pepper. Add the egg yolks, the ricotta and then the flour gradually. Season with pepper.
- In a large clean bowl whisk up the egg whites until light and fluffy. Gradually fold in the pepper mixture with a large metal spoon.
- Heat a non-stick frying pan or griddle on a medium heat and lightly grease the surface with an oiled paper. Drop a small ladle of batter into the frying pan and cook for about 1 minute. Turn over and when golden, remove and keep warm.
- Cut the scallions in strips and roll a few strips around the rolled pancakes. Serve with hot tomato sauce.

    A mixed salad, Corn on the Cob (page 59) or Vegetable Chili (page 48) can be served with these tasty pancakes.

Preparation Time: 20 minutes.
Cooking Time: 30 minutes, including sauce.

Frittata with Potatoes & Zucchini

Serves 4
4 medium potatoes, washed
4 tablespoon olive oil
1 medium onion, finely sliced
2 cloves garlic, crushed
2 zucchini, cut into thin slices
Salt and pepper, 1 teaspoon fresh rosemary
5 large eggs, beaten
1 tablespoon chopped parsley

- Boil the potatoes in their skins for 6 minutes, drain. Peel, if preferred, otherwise slice thinly with the skins.
- Heat the oil in a large frying pan and over a low heat cook the onions and garlic for about 4 minutes. Add the sliced potatoes and cook for 10 minutes on a medium heat, turning from time to time.
- Add the zucchini and continue cooking for 10 minutes, turning the vegetables from time to time. Sprinkle with rosemary.
- Beat the eggs in a bowl with salt and pepper. Mix with the vegetables.
- Heat the remaining oil in the pan and pour the mixture back into the pan over a medium heat. Keep pulling the frittata mixture back into the middle for the first few seconds.
- After about 5 minutes, either turn the frittata or place without turning under a hot broiler to cook the top. Sprinkle with chopped parsley.

Preparation Time: 18 minutes.
Cooking Time: 40 minutes.

Pepper Omelet

Serves 4-6
2 medium sweet red peppers, deseeded
1 medium sweet green pepper, deseeded
6 eggs
Salt and pepper
1 tablespoon oil
$1\frac{1}{4}$ cups light cream
$\frac{2}{3}$ cup sour cream
1 tablespoon chopped chives

- Preheat the oven to 400°F. Grease and line a round loose-bottomed cake tin, of the same diameter as your omelet pan, with aluminum foil.
- Cut the peppers into dice and blanch for 3 minutes in boiling water, keeping the colors separate. Drain.
- Beat up 3 eggs with 1 tablespoon cold water and add salt and pepper. Heat 1 teaspoon oil in an omelet pan, add half the red pepper and one-third of the egg mixture. Gently fry, pulling the egg mixture from the outside to the middle until set. Remove and turn out whole onto a plate. In the same way, make 2 more omelets with the green peppers.
- Beat the remaining 3 eggs together with the cream, chives and seasoning.
- Layer the omelets in the cake tin, pouring the egg and chive mixture between. Top with the rest of this mixture.

- Place the tin on a baking sheet and bake for 35 minutes. Cover the top with foil if it begins to look too brown. Serve cold in wedges with salad. An excellent picnic or packed lunch dish.

Preparation Time: 15 minutes.
Cooking Time: 50 minutes.

Lentil & Peanut Burgers

Lentil & Peanut Burgers

Serves 4-6

1 cup red lentils, washed
1 small onion, finely diced
1 cup peanuts
6 tablespoons fresh
wholewheat breadcrumbs
1 tablespoon chopped parsley
$\frac{1}{4}$ teaspoon dried oregano
Juice of half a lemon
$\frac{1}{2}$ teaspoon mild curry powder
(optional)
Salt and pepper

For the coating
1 beaten egg
1 cup wholewheat bread crumbs
1-2 tablespoons bran
Oil for frying

- Put the lentils in $2\frac{1}{2}$ cups cold water with a few drops of oil. Bring to the boil, cover with a lid and simmer for about 20 minutes until the lentils are soft and most of the water has been absorbed. On a low heat, beat the lentils until they form a creamy purée. Allow to cool and thicken.

- Chop the peanuts roughly in a food processor or blender. Mix into the lentils with the other ingredients. Allow to stand in the refrigerator for 15 minutes.

- Form into 8 rounded shapes and chill in the refrigerator for at least 30 minutes before cooking.

- Dip the burgers in egg and then into the crumbs mixed with bran. Again chill for at least 15 minutes before cooking for 5 minutes each side in hot oil.

    It is possible to use the mixture immediately but the burgers will be more difficult to handle.

Preparation Time: 50 minutes, including chilling.
Cooking Time: 30 minutes.

Variation
$\frac{1}{4}$-$\frac{1}{2}$ cup cheese may be added in place of a quarter of the peanuts. If using cheese, add a few drops of powdered mustard and a pinch of paprika.

Parsnip & Bean Crêpes

Serves 4

1 recipe Crêpes batter (page 63)
4 ounces parsnips, diced and cooked
7-ounce can lima beans
$\frac{1}{2}$ cup ricotta cheese
1 clove garlic, crushed
2 tablespoons lemon juice
$1\frac{1}{4}$ cups Tomato Sauce (page 36)

- Make the crêpes and keep warm in the oven. Wrap the stack of crêpes in foil to keep moist.
- Put the parsnips, lima beans, ricotta, garlic and lemon juice into a bowl and mix well together, mashing the beans and parsnips into the cheese.
- Preheat the oven to 400°F.
- Put a spoonful of mixture into each crêpe, fold in half, then in four. Arrange in an ovenproof dish, cover with foil and heat in the oven for 10 minutes. Serve with tomato sauce.

Preparation Time: 25 minutes.
Cooking Time: 15 minutes plus cooking time for tomato sauce.

Variations

Ricotta and Spinach Crêpes
Add 1 pound cooked drained spinach to the ricotta and use the mixture to fill the crêpes.

Mushroom Crêpes
Fry 2 cups sliced mushrooms in 1 tablespoon oil and 2 tablespoons butter or margarine. Mix with $1\frac{1}{4}$ cups Béchamel sauce (page 35).

Leek and Chive Crêpes
Clean and chop 2 leeks and fry in 2 tablespoons butter. Add 1 tablespoon chopped chives and mix well with $1\frac{1}{4}$ cups of Béchamel sauce. Fill the crêpes and reheat.

Curried Lentil Cakes

Serves 4-6

1 cup long-grain rice, lightly cooked
6 tablespoons oil
1 onion, finely chopped
1-2 cloves garlic, crushed
1-2 teaspoons curry paste

Leek & Chive Crêpes

$1\frac{1}{4}$ cups stock (page 12)
$\frac{1}{2}$ cup red lentils
1 cup mushrooms, chopped
$1\frac{1}{2}$ cups fresh brown breadcrumbs
1 tablespoon chopped parsley
1 tablespoon chopped coriander
1 egg, beaten
$\frac{1}{2}$ cup dried breadcrumbs

- Cook the rice (white or brown) in boiling water (10 minutes for white and 15 minutes for brown) and drain in a sieve.
- Heat the oil in a deep pan and gently cook the onion and garlic over a low heat to avoid browning. Add the curry paste and fry for a minute, mixing with the onion. Pour in the stock, stir in the rice and the lentils and simmer for 20 minutes until the lentils are tender.
- Add the mushrooms and cook for another 5 minutes. Allow to cool; most of the stock should now be absorbed.
- Mix in the breadcrumbs, parsley and coriander. Form into round cakes and put in the refrigerator or freezer for 20 minutes.
- Dip each cake in beaten egg and then in the dried breadcrumbs.
- Heat the remaining oil in a frying pan and fry the cakes for 3 minutes each side. Serve with a curry or tomato sauce.

Preparation Time: 20 minutes.
Cooking Time: 50 minutes.

Chili Beans

Serves 4
4 tablespoons olive oil
1 large onion, finely diced
2 cloves garlic, crushed
2 red chilis, finely diced
1 bay leaf, 1 bouquet garni
1 teaspoon cumin, 1 teaspoon oregano
16-ounce can plum tomatoes
16-ounce can red kidney beans, drained
1 pound textured vegetable protein granules
Salt and pepper
For the garnish
$2/_3$ cup sour cream
2 tablespoons chopped coriander

- Heat the oil and add the onion and garlic. Cook over a low heat for at least 4 minutes until the onion is transparent but not brown. Push to one side of the pan, then add the chilies. Add the textured vegetable protein granules and cook over a low heat for a few minutes, mixing with the onion and garlic.
- Turn into a saucepan or flameproof casserole and add the bay leaf, bouquet garni, cumin and oregano with the tomatoes and juice. Place over a medium heat and stir well to break the tomatoes down. Season with salt and pepper and simmer for 25 minutes. Check seasoning and, if not fiery enough, add a little chili powder or a few drops of chili sauce.
- Rinse the beans in a sieve or colander, add to the vegetables and stir gently. Simmer for about 15 minutes until all the ingredients are piping hot. Sprinkle with coriander.
- Serve with Soft Tortillas (page 91), Guacamole (page 22), and sour cream.

Preparation Time: 15 minutes.
Cooking Time: 45 minutes.

Rice & Cheese Quesadillas

Serves 4
2 tablespoons vegetable oil
1 onion, finely diced, 2 cloves garlic, crushed
1 cup chopped mushrooms
1 cup cooked rice
1 cup Tomato Sauce (page 36)
2-3 canned chili peppers, chopped (optional)
8 soft tortillas (page 91)
$1^1/_2$ cups grated cheese

- Heat the oil in a frying pan and gently cook the onion and garlic for 5 minutes. Add the mushrooms and continue cooking for another 4 minutes.
- Add the cooked rice and chilis to the mixture and stir well to mix.
- Preheat the oven to 400°F.
- Oil 4 baking pans and arrange one tortilla on the bottom of each. Top each with a quarter of the rice mixture. Place another tortilla on top and sprinkle with a quarter of the cheese. Brush with oil or tomato sauce.
- Cook for about 10-15 minutes until the cheese is melted, then cut each round into four. Serve with salad and guacamole or sour cream mixed with scallions.

Preparation Time: 10 -15 minutes.
Cooking Time: 25 minutes.

Variation
Corn kernels may be used in place of mushrooms. Extra cheese may be sprinkled on top.

Chili Beans in a tortilla

Country Baked Beans

Serves 8

1 pound navy beans, soaked
12 ounces red kidney beans, soaked
1 tablespoon oil
2 squares tempeh,
cut into strips
²/₃ cup dark brown sugar
3 tablespoons French mustard
2 tablespoons dark treacle or molasses
3 medium onions, chopped
1 pound tomatoes, skinned
16-ounce can plum tomatoes
3 carrots, diced
2 parsnips, diced

• Drain the beans into a colander and empty into a large saucepan. Cover the beans with cold water, bring to the boil and boil for 10 minutes. Reduce the heat and simmer for about 45 minutes until tender.

• Heat the oil and fry the tempeh. Preheat the oven to 375°F.

• Turn the cooked beans into a large casserole with the tempeh and all the other ingredients. Mix well with a wooden spoon.

• Turn the oven temperature down to 300°F. Bake the beans for 2 hours or more, stirring from time to time until they are a rich dark color. A little water or stock may be added if the beans look as if they are drying out.

Preparation Time: 20 minutes plus soaking time for beans.
Cooking Time: 2³/₄ hours.

Burghul Pilaf

Serves 4

¹/₄ cup butter or margarine
1 onion, finely chopped
8 ounces burghul (cracked) wheat
2 ounces dried apricots, chopped
¹/₂ cup raisins, rind and juice of 1 lemon
Salt and pepper, 2¹/₂ cups stock (page 12)
1 tablespoon chopped parsley

• Heat the butter or margarine in a large pan and cook the onion gently for 5 minutes until transparent.

• Add the burghul wheat and stir round in the pan for another minute. Add the raisins and the apricots with the rind and juice of the lemon, mix well and season.

• Pour in the stock and stir. Cover and simmer for about 15 minutes. When cooked, sprinkle with parsley. Serve in place of rice with a stir-fry or vegetable casserole.

Preparation Time: 10 minutes.
Cooking Time: 20 minutes.

Buffet Beans

Buffet Beans

Serves 4-8

1 pound green beans, cut into 1-inch lengths
8 ounces fava beans (optional)
1 8-ounce can red kidney beans, drained
1 tablespoon olive oil
1/2 cup Vinaigrette (page 38)
1 teaspoon French mustard
Salt and pepper
For the topping
1 cup crumbled blue cheese
1 cup cottage cheese

- Cook the green and fava beans separately in small amounts of boiling water until just tender. Drain well.
- Put all the beans, including the kidney beans, into a pan with 1 tablespoon olive oil. Stir the beans over a low heat until well mixed and warm.
- Remove from the heat and toss in the vinaigrette mixed with mustard. Season well and turn into a warm serving dish.
- Top the beans with the cottage cheese and sprinkle the crumbled blue cheese on top.

Preparation Time: 10 minutes.
Cooking Time: 10 minutes.

Nutty Bean Croquettes

Serves 4

8 ounces black-eyed beans, soaked overnight
2 cups buckwheat or
fresh white breadcrumbs
1/2 cup Brazil nuts, ground
3/4 cup grated cheese
1 clove garlic, crushed
1 teaspoon dried marjoram
1/2 teaspoon chili sauce
1 teaspoon chopped fresh parsley
For the coating
1 beaten egg
1 cup fresh white
or brown breadcrumbs
Oil for frying

- Drain the beans and put in a large saucepan of boiling water. Keep the beans boiling for 10 minutes then turn down the heat and simmer for 45 minutes or until tender.

- Drain the beans in a colander and rinse with cold water to cool. Mash the beans with a potato masher or put all the ingredients into the food processor. Mix well and chill in the refrigerator for 1 hour.
- Shape into 8 flat croquettes about 1/2 inch thick and chill for another hour.
- Dip the croquettes in egg and then into crumbs. Heat the oil in a frying pan and fry until golden brown on each side. Serve with a stir-fry or mixed salad.

Preparation Time: 10 minutes plus soaking and chilling times.
Cooking Time: 1 hour.

Canned beans can also be used for this recipe.

Nut Roast

Serves 4-6

2 carrots, peeled and chopped
2 parsnips, peeled and chopped
2 tablespoons vegetable oil
1 medium onion, diced
2 cloves garlic, crushed
1/2 cup butter
2 cups sliced mushrooms
2 cups mixed nuts
2 cups fresh breadcrumbs
1 teaspoon fresh rosemary
1/2 teaspoon thyme
1 egg
Salt and pepper
1 teaspoon soy sauce
2 tomatoes, peeled and sliced
1 tablespoon chopped parsley

- Cook the carrots and parsnips in salted water until tender. Drain well and let cool.
- Heat the oil and cook the onion and garlic over a low heat for a few minutes.
- In another pan heat three quarters of the butter and gently sauté the mushrooms for 5 minutes.
- Using a food processor, grind the nuts and herbs, tip into a bowl with the breadcrumbs, egg, seasoning and soy sauce. Mash or process the carrots and parsnips and add to the bowl.
- Preheat the oven to 350°F. Rub the remaining butter generously over a 2-pound loaf pan.
- Spoon half the mixture from the bowl into the pan. Cover with the mushrooms and sliced tomatoes. Finish with the remaining mixture. Cover with foil and cook for 1 hour. Allow to cool for 10-15 minutes

before turning out. Serve with Tomato Sauce (page 36).

Preparation Time: 25 minutes.
Cooking Time: 1 1/2 hours.

Bean Sausages

Makes 8

1 tablespoon oil
1 small onion, grated
1 carrot, grated
1 clove garlic, optional
8 ounces canned chick peas, drained
8 ounces canned navy beans, drained
1 teaspoon ground cumin
1 tablespoon tomato ketchup or paste
2 tablespoons tahini paste
Salt and pepper
1 tablespoon flour
1 1/2 cups fresh wholewheat breadcrumbs
2 tablespoons ground almonds

- Heat the oil in a small frying pan and add the onion, carrot and garlic. Fry gently for 4 minutes.
- Place the beans in a food processor and grind for a few seconds, then add the fried mixture, the cumin, ketchup, tahini paste and seasoning to form a coarse mix.
- With floured hands shape the mixture into 8 sausages. Beat the egg on a flat plate. Mix the breadcrumbs and ground almonds together in a dish.
- Dip each sausage into egg and then into the breadcrumb mixture. If time permits, chill for 20 minutes.
- Heat the oil in a deep frying pan and cook the sausages for about 4 minutes until crisp and golden.

Preparation Time: 20 minutes.
Cooking Time: 12 minutes.

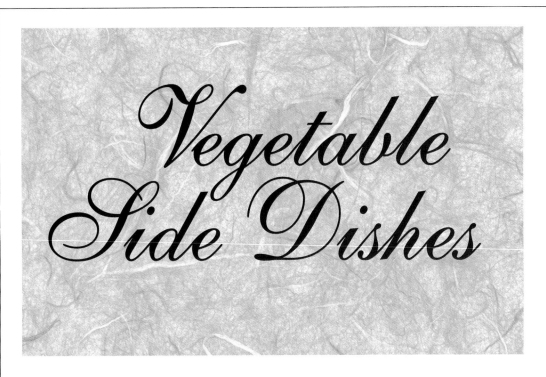

Vegetable Side Dishes

Broccoli Spears with Vegetable Rings

Serves 4

1 pound broccoli spears
1 sweet red pepper
1 red onion, cut into rings
1 tablespoon butter or low fat spread
1 teaspoon red wine vinegar
1/2 teaspoon dried rosemary or
1 teaspoon fresh
2 tablespoons low fat yogurt (optional)

• Prepare the broccoli spears by trimming away any rough parts of the stalks with a potato peeler. Deseed the pepper, cut into thin rings and rinse under cold water.

• Arrange the broccoli and onion rings in a steamer. Put about 1 inch of water in the pan – the steaming basket should not touch the water. Bring to the boil, cover and steam for about 4 minutes.

• Uncover, add the peppers and cook for another 4 minutes or until the vegetables are nearly tender but still retaining their shape and texture. Arrange on a heated serving dish.

• Melt the butter or low fat spread in a small pan and add the vinegar and rosemary. Drizzle over the vegetables and serve accompanied by yogurt in a separate dish.

Preparation Time: 10 minutes.
Cooking Time: 12 minutes.

Medley of Hot Green Vegetables

Serves 4

1/3 cup raisins
6 tablespoons fresh orange juice
1 tablespoon soy sauce
4 tablespoons olive oil, 1 onion, finely diced
2 cloves garlic, crushed
8 ounces broccoli spears
4 ounces snow peas
1 pound fresh spinach, washed and dried
1/2 cup pine nuts, toasted
2 teaspoons grated orange rind
Black pepper

• Place the raisins in a bowl together with the orange juice and soy sauce, and leave them to plump up for about 40 minutes.

• Heat the oil in a wok or large frying pan and cook the onion and garlic over a medium heat. Stir until the onion is soft.

• Raise the heat and add the broccoli and stir for 2 minutes. Add the snow peas and spinach leaves. Toss the vegetables over the heat for 2 minutes then add the pine nuts with the orange rind and a good shake of black pepper.

• Stir well for 1 minute, taste for seasoning and serve immediately.

Preparation Time: 10 minutes plus 40 minutes soaking time for raisins.
Cooking Time: 6 minutes.

Caponata

Serves 4

2 medium eggplants,
sliced and cut into quarters
Salt
2/3 cup olive oil
4 medium onions, cut into rings
2 cloves garlic, crushed
2 stalks celery, thinly sliced
1 cup green olives, pitted and halved
16-ounce can tomatoes with half their juice
Black pepper
1 tablespoon sugar
4 tablespoons wine vinegar
2 tablespoons capers, drained and chopped
1 tablespoon fresh parsley
1 tablespoon fresh basil

• Arrange the quartered slices of eggplant on a tray and sprinkle with salt. Allow to stand for about 30 minutes. Rinse the eggplant and dry on kitchen paper.

• Heat the oil and add the eggplant pieces. Cook, turning in the pan, until golden brown. Remove from the pan and lower the heat. Add the onions and garlic to the frying pan and allow to cook, stirring from time to time until soft.

• Add the remaining vegetables and simmer for 25 minutes. Sprinkle in the sugar, vinegar, capers and herbs. Serve with vegetable flans, pasties or rissoles.

Preparation Time: 10 minutes plus standing time.
Cooking Time: 35 minutes.

Jerusalem Artichokes with Béchamel Sauce

Serves 4

2 pounds Jerusalem artichokes
2 tablespoons vinegar
1 1/4 cups Béchamel Sauce (page 35)
2 tablespoons whipping cream (optional)
2 tablespoons chopped parsley

• Peel the artichokes, removing the larger knobs, and cut into even-sized pieces. To avoid discoloration, immerse in water acidulated with vinegar until ready to cook.

- Prepare the sauce and add the cream if using.
- Drain the artichokes, then boil or steam until tender. Turn into a heated serving dish.
- Add half the parsley to the warm sauce and pour onto the artichokes. Sprinkle with the remaining parsley.

Preparation Time: 15 minutes.
Cooking Time: 25 minutes.

Artichokes, fresh from the garden, are so good that this dish is a feast in itself. Serve with wholewheat pasties or vegetable fritters.

Artichokes can also be served with Hollandaise sauce and the larger ones can be cut up and cooked in oil like French fries.

Jerusalem Artichoke and Potato Purée
To serve 4

Cook 1 pound artichokes as above. Boil 12 ounces potatoes (after peeling) in salted water until tender. Put the artichokes and potatoes through a ricer or wide meshed sieve, adding a knob of butter, some pepper and 3 tablespoons cream. Mix well together, reheat and serve piping hot.

Jerusalem Artichokes with Red Pepper Dressing

Cook the artichokes as above. Meanwhile, blanch a large deseeded sweet red pepper for 5 minutes in boiling salted water. Purée the pepper in a blender or food processor with 1 small chili pepper, 2 tablespoons olive oil, and 1 clove of crushed garlic (optional). Serve with the hot Jerusalem artichokes for an interesting combination of flavors.

Jerusalem Artichokes with Red Pepper Dressing

Creamed Leeks

Serves 4
4 leeks, washed, 2 tablespoons butter
Salt and pepper, juice and rind of 1 lemon
$^2/_3$ cup light cream
1 tablespoon chopped parsley

- Shred the leeks finely with a sharp knife or use the food processor.
- Heat the butter in a pan over a low heat, add the leeks and cook over a medium heat, turning them around, for about 5 minutes.
- Add seasoning, lemon rind and juice and stir well for about 1 minute. Lastly stir in the cream and sprinkle with chopped parsley.

Preparation Time: 6 minutes.
Cooking Time: 6 minutes.

Variation
Add the juice and rind of 1 orange with 1 teaspoon lemon juice for an unusual flavor.

Spiced Turnips

Serves 4
1 pound young turnips, washed
$1^1/_2$ cups salsify, peeled and sliced
$1^1/_2$ cups okra, trimmed
2 tablespoons butter
1 small piece of fresh ginger, grated
2 tablespoons grain mustard
2 tablespoons yogurt

- Cook the turnips and salsify in boiling salted water for 30 minutes, adding the okra for the last 10 minutes of cooking time.
- Drain the vegetables and run under a cold tap.
- Heat the butter in a frying pan and add the ginger, turnip, salsify and okra. Toss over the heat for 2 minutes, then add the mustard. Toss again and add the yogurt just before serving. Garnish with toasted cashew nuts.

Preparation Time: 10 minutes.
Cooking Time: 35 minutes.

Braised Red Cabbage

Serves 4
1 x 3-pound head of red cabbage, washed, trimmed and cut into thin slices
4 tablespoons vegetable oil
2 tablespoons sugar
2 tablespoons vinegar
$^2/_3$ cup water, 2 crisp eating apples
$^1/_4$ cup red currant jelly

- Preheat the oven to 325°F.
- Mix the oil in an ovenproof casserole with the sugar, vinegar and water. Bring to the boil on top of the stove. Add the cabbage and cover with a tight lid.
- Place in the oven for 1 hour, remove and stir. Add a little more water if necessary. Return to the oven for a further 30 minutes then add the cored, sliced apple and return to the oven for another 20-30 minutes.

Preparation Time: 10 minutes.
Cooking time: 2 hours.

Broccoli in Cheese Sauce

Serves 4 as a side dish or 2 as a main course
1½ pounds broccoli, washed
2 cups Béchamel Sauce (page 35)
1 tablespoon butter
2 tablespoons thick cream
Salt and pepper
½ teaspoon grated nutmeg
1 cup grated Swiss cheese

- Heat 2 inches of water in a large saucepan. Add the broccoli spears and cook for 5-6 minutes until crisp.
- Heat the oven to 350°F and prepare the sauce.
- Drain the broccoli and arrange in a buttered ovenproof dish.
- Mix the cream into the sauce and season well. Pour over the sauce and sprinkle with nutmeg. Sprinkle the cheese evenly on top and bake in the oven for 20 minutes.

Preparation Time: 10 minutes.
Cooking Time: 40 minutes including time for making sauce.

Variations

Broccoli with Hollandaise Sauce
Another excellent vegetable side dish is crisply cooked broccoli topped with Hollandaise sauce (page 37).

Cauliflower in Cheese Sauce
Cook a large cauliflower cut into florets or leave whole, if preferred, when it will need 15 minute's cooking time. Florets take about 8 minutes.

2 hard-boiled eggs can be chopped and sprinkled over the cauliflower before adding the sauce and cooking as for broccoli to make a hearty vegetarian meal.

Country-Style Peas

Serves 4
6 ounces baby onions,
fresh or frozen
2 cups frozen or fresh shelled peas
2 tablespoons butter
1 cup vegetable stock (page 12)
Salt and pepper
1 tablespoon chopped parsley (optional)

- If using fresh onions, peel and dry on kitchen paper. Heat half the butter in a pan, add the onions and toss in the butter for about 1 minute.
- Add the peas, stock and seasoning and gently stir to mix.
- Cover with a lid and simmer on a low heat until the vegetables are tender, about 10 minutes. Drain if necessary and add the remaining butter to the pan, shaking well to mix.
- Turn into a warm serving dish and sprinkle with parsley.

Preparation Time: 2-20 minutes according to type of onions and peas used.
Cooking time: 10 minutes.

LEFT: *Spiced Turnips*
RIGHT: *Spinach with Tomatoes (p 75)*

Bean Sprout Medley

Serves 4

4 carrots, cooked and cut into julienne strips
1 tablespoon olive oil
$^2/_3$ cup bean sprouts
4 pineapple rings, fresh or canned, diced
8-oz can lima beans, drained
Sprigs of marjoram

• Cook the carrots in boiling salted water and cut into thin strips.
• Heat the oil in a pan and toss in the bean sprouts, pineapple, lima beans and carrots. Turn the vegetables around with a fork until they are heated through. Serve.

Preparation Time: 10 minutes.
Cooking Time: 15 minutes.

Green Stir-Fry

Serves 4

1 pound broccoli spears
2 tablespoons sesame oil
4 scallions, finely chopped
2 cloves garlic, crushed
8 ounces snow peas
8 ounces thin green beans
2 ounces young spinach leaves,
washed and drained
1 orange, peeled and cut into segments

For the seasoning

2 tablespoons hoisin sauce
1 tablespoon sesame seeds
1 tablespoon parsley, chopped
1 tablespoon chives, chopped

• Break the broccoli into florets and place in a pan of boiling water for about 2 minutes. Drain into a colander.
• Heat the oil, add the scallions, garlic, snow peas, and the green beans. Stir well for about 2 minutes. Add the spinach and orange segments gradually.
• Add the hoisin sauce, stir well, then sprinkle on the seeds and herbs. Serve piping hot. This dish is excellent with Smoked Tofu Kebabs (page 52).

Preparation Time: 10 minutes.
Cooking Time: 6 minutes.

OPPOSITE: *Potato Cakes*
BELOW: *Bean Sprout Medley*

Potato Cakes

Makes 8
8 ounces potatoes, well scrubbed
4 ounces parsnips, well scrubbed
1 teaspoon salt
Oil for frying

- Cook the unpeeled potatoes in boiling salted water for 5 minutes, add the parsnips, and cook for a further 5 minutes. Drain, and allow to cool down.
- When comfortable to handle, coarsely grate the vegetables and mix them well together. Form into 8 cakes or patties, flattening them between the hands.
- Generously oil a griddle or thick skillet and fry the cakes for 3 minutes on each side or until golden brown. Sprinkle generously with chopped chives. Serve with fried eggs, mushrooms and tomatoes.

Steamed Zucchini with Spinach Purée

Serves 4
4 zucchini, cut into rings
1 pound fresh baby spinach, washed
1 small piece of fresh ginger, grated
$1/2$ cup low fat yogurt
$1/2$ teaspoon cumin
Salt and pepper

- Steam the zucchini, and spinach with the ginger, separately. Keep the zucchini warm in a serving dish.
- Purée the spinach with the cumin in a blender or food processor together with the low fat yogurt. Season well.
- Spoon the purée over the zucchini.

Preparation Time: 10 minutes.
Cooking Time: 10 minutes.

Spinach with Tomatoes

Serves 4
$2^1/2$ pounds fresh spinach, washed
$1^1/4$ cups Basic White or Béchamel Sauce
(pages 34-35)
1 onion, chopped
4 large ripe tomatoes, skinned
Freshly grated nutmeg
Salt and pepper,
$1/2$ cup grated cheese

- Remove stalks from the spinach and steam for 5 minutes, or cook in 2 tablespoons boiling water for 4-5 minutes. Drain in a colander and squeeze out excess moisture. Roughly chop.
- Lightly fry the onion and mix with the spinach. Season and sprinkle with nutmeg. Place in a heatproof dish.
- Cut the tomatoes into thick rings and arrange over the spinach. Pour the sauce over the tomatoes. Sprinkle with grated cheese and parsley.
- Can be briefly placed in a hot oven to slightly melt the cheese, if required.

Preparation Time: 15 minutes.
Cooking Time: 20 minutes.

Lima Beans with Tomatoes

Serves 4
16-ounce can lima beans, drained
2 pounds plum or ripe tomatoes, skinned
Salt and pepper, 4 tablespoons olive oil
4 cloves garlic, thinly sliced
12 sage leaves

- Put the drained beans into a bowl. Skin the tomatoes, chop them, mix into the beans and season well.
- Heat 3 tablespoons olive oil and add the garlic and sage leaves. Fry for about 2 minutes. Add the beans and tomatoes and simmer gently for 15 minutes.
- Serve sprinkled with the remaining olive oil and warm wholewheat bread.

Preparation Time: 10 minutes.
Cooking Time: 20 minutes.

If using dried beans, soak them overnight in cold water. Bring them to the boil in a pan of water, drain and refill before cooking for $1^1/2$ hours. Cook for 15 minutes with the tomatoes and other ingredients.

Pasta

Pasta is an instant energy food, beloved of athletes and the ideal accompaniment to an endless variety of vegetarian dishes. There are times when freshly made pasta, which can be bought or made at home – either by hand or with a pasta machine – is the order of the day. At other times dried pasta may be appropriate, having a unique quality all its own. Although an acquired taste, wholewheat pasta is widely available and provides that all-important extra fiber, an vital constituent of the healthy diet. Vegetable sauces and pasta make an ideal marriage and pasta goes equally well with vegetable casseroles and roasted vegetables.

Cooking pasta

Perfectly cooked pasta is delicious eaten by itself with a sprinkling of black pepper, a little butter or olive oil and grated Parmesan cheese. It is simple to cook but it is important to remember a few basic rules as badly cooked pasta is not at all pleasant to eat.

It should be cooked *al dente* which means 'to the tooth'. This means it must still retain a certain bite or slight chewiness of texture after cooking. Follow the cooking times suggested on commercial brands and test before draining by biting a strand between the teeth.

Always use a large saucepan as pasta needs room to cook; if squashed into a small container it will boil over and create a mess. You will need 1 quart of water for every 4 ounces of pasta. To cook 1 pound of dried spaghetti the pan really needs to hold 4 quarts of water. Many people do not possess such a large saucepan, therefore it is advisable to cook only 8 ounces of pasta at a time. Keep the first batch warm while the other half is cooking, then place all the pasta into boiling water to reheat before draining again and serving.

•

Bring the water to a rolling boil before adding the pasta. Add 1 teaspoon salt to every quart of water.

•

Add the pasta gradually, feeding it into the pan and keeping the water boiling. Stir round with a fork to prevent strands from sticking together.

•

Use the cooking times as a guide and taste a strand or piece at least 1-2 minutes before the time is up. Bite through the pasta and decide whether or not it is to your taste.

•

Drain into a colander and, if liked, melt a knob of butter in the pan and then return the pasta to it with a shake of freshly ground pepper and a little grated nutmeg. Toss in the buttery mixture and serve piping hot.

•

A colorful sauce sitting on top of pasta looks pretty but will be much more tasty if it is well mixed into the pasta before serving with a sprinkling of grated cheese. Use $2^1/_2$ cups sauce to 1 pound of pasta.

•

2 ounces dried pasta provides a small portion, 3 ounces makes a good average serving and hearty appetites will require 4 ounces.

Pasta Dough

Makes 1 pound
1 pound all-purpose flour
$^1/_2$ teaspoon salt
2 eggs, 1 tablespoon olive oil
5-7 tablespoons warm water

• Sift the flour and salt onto a clean work surface or pastry board. Make a well in the center of the flour.
• Beat the eggs in a cup and add gradually to the center well. Draw the flour in and over the eggs as you mix. Add the oil and a little water and mix with a spatula. Pull the flour over the soft dough in the middle and mix with floured hands until you have a smooth paste.
• Knead the dough for a few minutes, cover with plastic film and rest in the refrigerator for 10-20 minutes.
• Roll out the dough with a rolling pin into flat sheets to make lasagna, cannelloni and ravioli or into strips suitable for feeding into a pasta making machine.

Preparation time: 30 minutes.
Cooking Time: Thin strips 2-3 minutes. Filled shapes 7-8 minutes depending on size.

Variations
Spinach Pasta
Substitute 2 tablespoons spinach purée for 2 tablespoons water.
Tomato Pasta
Substitute 1 tablespoon tomato paste for 1 tablespoon water.

Tagliatelli with Ricotta

Serves 4
1 cup ricotta cheese
3 tablespoons low fat cream
Salt and freshly ground pepper
$^1/_2$ teaspoon paprika
$^1/_2$ teaspoon cinnamon
1 teaspoon sugar, 1 pound tagliatelle
For the garnish
Sprigs of parsley

• Mix the cheese, cream, seasonings, cinnamon and sugar together in a bowl.

Tagliatelli with Pumpkin

• Cook the pasta in boiling salted water (3-4 minutes if fresh and 10-12 if dried). Drain the pasta in a colander and shake out moisture.

• Tip the pasta into the bowl with the cheese mixture. Mix well and return to the saucepan. Stir over a low heat and serve garnished with parsley.

Preparation time: 5 minutes.
Cooking Time: 10 minutes.

Variation

Tagliatelle with Pumpkin

Cook 1 pound pumpkin, drain and purée or mash. Omit $^3/_4$ cup ricotta cheese and proceed as above.

Mixed Vegetable Lasagna

Serves 4-6

3³/₄ cups Béchamel Sauce (page 35)
2¹/₂ cups Tomato Sauce (page 36)
1 large eggplant, sliced, 6 tablespoons oil
2 zucchini, sliced, 1¹/₂ cups mushrooms, sliced
1 sweet green pepper, deseeded and chopped
8 large sheets lasagna or 16 small, cooked
(unless the non-cook variety)
¹/₂ cup cheese, grated,
¹/₂ cup fresh breadcrumbs

- Make up the two sauces and prepare the vegetables. Slice the eggplant and put in a colander or on a flat plate. Sprinkle with salt and allow to stand for 30 minutes.
- Heat half the oil in a large pan and fry the zucchini on both sides over a medium heat. Drain on kitchen paper. Add the mushrooms and cook for about 3 minutes. Drain.
- Place the green pepper in a small saucepan of boiling water for about 2 minutes. Drain well.
- Rinse the salt from the eggplant slices and drain well, dry with kitchen paper. Fry the eggplant slices in the remaining oil in batches, drain on kitchen paper.
- Preheat the oven to 350°F.
- Using a large square or oblong ovenproof dish, spoon some tomato sauce over the bottom and cover with a little Béchamel sauce. Place the first layer of lasagna on top with a little tomato sauce and then arrange half the vegetables on top of that making sure that they are evenly distributed. Cover with the Béchamel sauce.
- Arrange the next layer of lasagna, spread half the tomato sauce and the remainder of the vegetables topped with the sauce.
- Cover with the last layer of lasagna, topped with the remaining tomato sauce and covered with the Béchamel sauce.
- Sprinkle on the cheese, then the crumbs and cook in the oven for 35-40 minutes until golden brown.

Preparation time: 45 minutes.
Cooking Time: 35- 40 minutes.

Variation
Spinach and Ricotta Lasagna
Use 2¹/₂ cups Béchamel sauce with 2 pounds cooked spinach, seasoned with nutmeg, salt and pepper and 1 pound ricotta cheese. Layer the spinach, ricotta and lasagna in the same way as the vegetables are laid in the previous recipe. Scatter a little ricotta on top of the final layer.

Spinach & Ricotta Lasagna

Ravioli

Serves 4

1 pound Pasta Dough (page 76)

1. Ricotta and Parmesan Filling

1 cup ricotta cheese
2 tablespoons grated Parmesan cheese
2 tablespoons chopped parsley
1 tablespoon fresh breadcrumbs
Salt and pepper
1 egg, beaten

2. Ricotta and Spinach Filling

1 cup ricotta cheese
1 cup fresh or frozen spinach,
cooked and well drained
2 tablespoons parsley
1 tablespoon fresh breadcrumbs
Salt and pepper
1 egg, beaten

- Make up the pasta dough and set it to rest while the filling(s) is made.
- Cut the dough into circles with a 2-inch pastry cutter. Brush the edges of the circles with water and arrange the stuffing on one side. Fold the dough over the filling and seal by pinching the edges together with a fork.
- Cook in a large pan of boiling salted water for about 6 minutes or until *al dente*. Serve with Tomato Sauce (page 36).

Preparation time: 30 minutes.
Cooking Time: 6 minutes.

Variation

- Divide the dough into two pieces. Roll out one of the pieces as thinly as possible into a rectangular shape. Mark out $1\frac{1}{2}$-inch squares lightly on the dough.
- Place one teaspoon of filling in the center of each square.
- Roll out the other half of the dough to the same size. Wet the dough round each mound of filling with a pastry brush. Cover with the second piece of dough and cut round the squares with a pastry wheel or a sharp knife. Place on a flat tray and cover with plastic film if not cooking immediately.

ABOVE: *Ravioli*

Pasta with Spicy Vegetables

Serves 4

2 cups spinach, cooked and drained
2 sweet yellow peppers, deseeded
4 tablespoons olive oil
1 onion, diced
1-2 cloves garlic, crushed
2 tablespoons basil, chopped
$\frac{1}{2}$ teaspoon paprika
salt and pepper
4 tablespoons white wine
1 pound dried pasta shapes
$\frac{1}{2}$ cup grated pecorino cheese

- Cook the spinach and allow to drain well. Squeeze all excess water out by hand.

Blanch the peppers in boiling water for 2 minutes, drain and allow to cool.

- Heat 3 tablespoons oil and gently cook the onion and garlic for about 3 minutes. Dice the pepper and add to the onion with the basil and paprika. Pour in the white wine and 4 tablespoons water. Season and allow to simmer for 2 minutes.
- Stir in the spinach, cover and simmer gently for 10 minutes.
- Meanwhile cook the pasta *al dente*, drain in a colander and mix with the vegetables in a saucepan or a heated bowl.
- Sprinkle with the remaining olive oil and the cheese. Serve piping hot.

Preparation time: 15 minutes.
Cooking Time: 20 minutes.

Cannelloni

Serves 4

8 sheets of lasagna, fresh or dried

For the Filling

$1\frac{1}{2}$ cups cooked spinach

$\frac{1}{2}$ cup ricotta cheese

Salt and pepper

1 tablespoon fresh breadcrumbs

1 tablespoon Parmesan cheese

1 teaspoon marjoram

Freshly grated nutmeg

For the Sauces

$1\frac{1}{4}$ cups Tomato Sauce (page 36)

$1\frac{1}{4}$ cups Béchamel Sauce (page 35)

To finish

$\frac{1}{2}$ cup grated cheese

1 tablespoon fresh breadcrumbs

- For home-made pasta, see page 76. If bought, and whether fresh or dried, follow the manufacturer's instructions for cooking on the pack. The 'no-cook' type of dried lasagna can be placed in a pan of boiling water for about 2 minutes until soft enough to handle. Drain and lay out on a flat tray.

- Pour the tomato sauce into the bottom of a shallow, rectangular ovenproof dish.

- Preheat the oven to 350°F.

- Mix all the filling ingredients together in a bowl to make a creamy mixture, making sure that they are evenly distributed.

- Stuff the pasta by putting the filling in a large piping bag with a plain piping tube or use lightly floured hands to form the filling into sausage shapes.

- Place a roll of stuffing about $\frac{3}{4}$ inch in diameter along the center of each strip of lasagna, roll over to form a tube and cut into two. Lay seam sides down in the tomato sauce and repeat until you have made 16 rolls.

- Pour over the Béchamel sauce and sprinkle with cheese and breadcrumbs. Bake for 25-30 minutes until golden brown.

Preparation time: 45 minutes.

Cooking Time: 30 minutes.

These times include making the sauces. Dried cannelloni shells are available, though rather fragile. They are larger than the rolls described here, therefore allow only 2-3 per

person. Filling these shells is difficult without using a piping bag. However a spoon can be used when it is best to fill from each end to meet in the middle.

Pasta with Putanesca Sauce

Serves 4

2 tablespoons oil
1 onion, diced, 1 carrot, diced
2 pounds plum tomatoes, skinned or
1 16-oz can plum tomatoes
1 bay leaf, 1 bouquet garni
4-5 basil leaves, salt and pepper
6 tablespoons white wine
1 tablespoon capers
$^1\!/_2$ cup black olives, pitted
3-4 drops Tabasco sauce
1 tablespoon chopped parsley
12 ounces pasta
1 tablespoon olive oil
Parmesan cheese

- Heat the oil in a deep saucepan and cook the onions gently over a low heat for about 3 minutes. Add the diced or grated carrot and continue cooking for 5 minutes.
- Add the tomatoes, bay leaf, bouquet garni, basil, seasoning and white wine. Bring to the boil and simmer for 30 minutes.
- Remove the bay leaf and bouquet garni. Sieve, blend or process the mixture and return to the saucepan with the capers, black olives and Tabasco sauce. Reheat gently and add parsley just before serving
- Cook the pasta, depending on type, drain and mix with oil and then sauce before serving. Hand round a bowl of Parmesan cheese separately.

Preparation Time: 15 minutes.
Cooking Time: 35 minutes.

LEFT: *Cannelloni*
RIGHT: *Making a pesto sauce by hand*

Pasta with Pesto

Serves 4

1 pound penne or other pasta shapes
2 tablespoons olive oil
$1^1\!/_2$ cups oyster mushrooms, sliced
12 cherry tomatoes, halved
For the Pesto Sauce
1 cup basil leaves, 2 cloves garlic, crushed
Salt, $^1\!/_2$ cup pine kernels
$^1\!/_2$ cup Parmesan cheese
8 tablespoons olive oil

- Process the basil leaves in a blender or food processor for a few seconds, add the garlic and gradually pour in the oil with the machine running.
- Add the pine kernels and then the Parmesan cheese. The mixture will be thick and creamy.
- Heat 2 tablespoons oil in a frying pan and cook the mushrooms and halved tomatoes for about 5 minutes over a medium heat.
- Cook the pasta and drain well. Return to the saucepan with half the pesto, the mushrooms and tomatoes and mix well. Serve with more pesto spooned on top of each portion.

Preparation Time: 5 minutes by machine, 12 minutes by hand.
Cooking Time: 15 minutes.
Pesto sauce is often served alone with pasta.

Variation
Winter Pesto
Half basil and half parsley makes an excellent sauce when fresh basil is expensive and difficult to get in the winter months. To make the sauce by hand, use a pestle and mortar. Grind the basil with the garlic, salt and pine nuts, then gradually mix in the oil and cheese.

Fettuccini Roma

Serves 4
1 pound fettuccini
$^1/_4$ cup butter
$^1/_2$ teaspoon freshly grated nutmeg
$^1/_2$ cup light cream
Salt and pepper
1 cup Parmesan cheese, grated

- Cook the fettucini – it will only take 2-3 minutes if using fresh.
  Drain the pasta into a colander.
- Melt the butter in the saucepan, add the nutmeg and half the cream, stir until the mixture is shiny and bubbly.
- Tip the fettuccini into the pan and stir well. Add the remaining cream and cheese alternately, stirring to mix.

Preparation Time: 5 minutes.
Cooking Time: 5 minutes.

Pasta with Roquefort

Serves 4-6
$2^1/_2$ cups Béchamel Sauce (page 35)
$^1/_2$ cup Roquefort cheese, crumbled
Freshly ground pepper
$^1/_2$ teaspoon French mustard
Pinch of cayenne pepper
1-$1^1/_4$ pounds pasta

- Make up a well flavored Béchamel sauce and add the cheese to the sauce along with the seasonings. Reheat over a gentle heat.
- Cook the pasta and mix well with the sauce just before serving.

Preparation Time:15 minutes.
Cooking Time: 20 minutes.

Variation
Other blue cheeses can be used for this sauce.

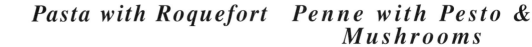

Penne with Pesto & Mushrooms

Serves 4
12 ounces penne
2 tablespoons butter
12 ounces oyster mushrooms, sliced
8 ounces cherry tomatoes, halved
Freshly ground black pepper
1 cup Pesto Sauce (page 81)

- Cook the penne *al dente*, about 12 minutes. Drain. Return to the pan over a low heat and mix with the pesto sauce.
- Meanwhile, lightly sauté the mushrooms and tomatoes in butter for about 5 minutes.
- Serve the penne on warm plates mixed with the mushrooms and tomatoes.

Preparation Time: 15 minutes including making the pesto sauce.
Cooking time: 12-15 minutes.

Penne with Two Cheeses

Serves 4
4 tablespoons olive oil
2 medium onions, thinly sliced
2 sweet red peppers, deseeded and thinly sliced
1 cup pitted black olives, halved
2 tablespoons chopped basil
Salt and pepper,
12 ounces penne
4 ounces Mozzarella cheese, cut into cubes
4 ounces Fontina cheese, grated

- Heat the oil in a large frying pan, add the onions and cook gently for about 4 minutes. Add the peppers and continue cooking for a further 6 minutes
- Meanwhile, cook the pasta *al dente* in boiling water. Drain in a colander.
- Add the pasta to the frying pan over a low heat with the olives and basil. Stir in the cheeses carefully and season to taste.
- Spoon the pasta onto warm plates.

Preparation Time: 20 minutes.
Cooking time: 10-15 minutes.

Potato Gnocchi

Serves 4
1 pound peeled potatoes, sliced
2 cups all-purpose flour
Salt and pepper
2 tablespoons melted butter

- Cook the potatoes in boiling, salted water. Drain well before sieving or ricing into a bowl.
- Sift the flour with $\frac{1}{2}$ teaspoon salt into the bowl and mix with the potatoes. Add a little pepper and the melted butter.
- Turn onto a floured board and knead lightly until an elastic dough is formed.
- Divide the mixture into 1-inch pieces. Twist and pull ends towards you to shape. If possible leave to rest for 20 minutes in the refrigerator.
- Butter an ovenproof dish, sprinkle with sage and arrange some slices of Mozzarella on the bottom. Preheat the oven to 400°F.
- Prepare a large pan of fast-boiling salted water and drop in the gnocchi. Cook for about 10 minutes. Lift the gnocchi out with a slotted spoon.
- Place the drained gnocchi onto the dish and bake in the oven for 15-20 minutes or until golden brown.
- Serve piping hot with Tomato Sauce (page 36).

Preparation Time: 30 minutes including resting time.
Cooking Time: 10 minutes.

Variation
Pumpkin, squash and spinach can be used in place of potato for flavoring. Plain gnocchi can be made with fine semolina instead of flour and can be deep fried.

Tomato & Olive Gnocchi

Serves 4
2 tablespoons butter or margarine
2 cups mushrooms, sliced
1 garlic clove, crushed
2 scallions, finely chopped
6 large ripe tomatoes, skinned
1 tablespoon chopped parsley
$\frac{1}{2}$ cup olives, pitted and chopped
1 recipe Potato Gnocchi (see above)
1 cup grated cheese

- Heat the butter or margarine in a large frying pan and fry the mushrooms and garlic over a moderate heat.
- Oil an ovenproof dish and arrange the mushrooms on the bottom. Sprinkle with the scallions.
- Arrange the sliced tomatoes on top of the mushrooms, sprinkle with parsley and chopped olives.
- Preheat the oven to 350°F.
- Form the gnocchi into squares and use it to cover the vegetables in the dish. Sprinkle with cheese.
- Bake in the oven for 25 minutes and serve piping hot.

Preparation Time: 25 minutes.
Cooking Time: 40 minutes.

OPPOSITE: *Penne with Pesto & Mushrooms*
BELOW: *Tomato & Olive Gnocchi*

Rice

Rice is one of the oldest foods known to mankind and forms the staple diet of at least half the human race making it undeniably one of the world's most important foods. Rice is an essential part of most oriental cuisines – Indian, Korean, Chinese, Indonesian and Japanese – and many of the most interesting ways of cooking it originate from those cultures.

As rice requires so little preparation and is so easily stored, it is the ideal food for busy cooks and a bonus for vegetarians. There is no wastage and any left-overs can be quickly turned into a main meal with vegetables or a tasty salad. Do make sure you read the pack instructions and ensure that the rice you are buying is the correct type for the dish you have in mind.

Main types of rice

There are countless varieties of rice of which there are two basic types – long-grain (which includes Patna, Basmati and American long-grain) and short-/medium-grain (Italian Arborio, Carolina, Java), useful for risottos and puddings. Brown rice can be any of these: it is rice which has been hulled but without depriving it of its bran, thereby making it higher in fiber and more nutritious. Other off-spins are ground rice and rice flour, useful for baking and puddings and wild rice which is not a true rice but the seed of an aquatic plant grown in the United States.

To cook long-grain rice

For 8 ounces long-grain rice, use $\frac{1}{2}$ teaspoon salt and $2\frac{1}{2}$ cups water. Wash the rice in a sieve. Boil the water in a large saucepan, add the salt and then the rice. Allow the water to return to the boil for 1 minute, then simmer the rice for about 12 minutes when most of the water will be absorbed. Cover and allow to stand for 10 minutes. Lightly fluff up the rice with a fork.

If buying pre-fluffed or part-processed rice, follow the cooking instructions on the side of the pack.

Brown rice or a mixture of brown, white or wild rices will take longer to cook.

Mushroom Risotto

Pilau Rice

Serves 4
1¼ cups long-grain or Basmati rice
2 tablespoons oil
1 onion, peeled and finely chopped
1 clove garlic, crushed
½ teaspoon cumin
¼ teaspoon turmeric
½ teaspoon fresh chili pepper
¼ teaspoon ground coriander
1 teaspoon salt
2 cups vegetable stock (page 12)

• Wash the rice and allow it to soak in cold water for about 20 minutes. Drain in a sieve then shake well to remove excess water.
• Heat the oil and fry the onion and garlic over a medium heat until golden brown.
• Add the drained rice and stir over a low heat. Add the cumin, turmeric, chili and coriander.
• Add the salt to the boiling stock and gradually add to the rice, stirring all the time. Bring the pan to the boil and allow the rice to simmer, covered, over a low heat for 15-20 minutes or until tender. Fluff up the rice with a fork before serving.

Preparation Time: 25 minutes.
Cooking Time: 30 minutes.

Variation
Cashew nuts and sultanas can be added to this mixture near the end of the cooking time.

Mushroom Risotto

If fresh wild mushrooms are available, use a mixture of them to make a superb risotto.

Serves 4
1 tablespoon olive oil
4 tablespoons butter
1 onion, finely chopped
1½ cups risotto
(arborio) rice
1 cup button mushrooms, chopped
1 cup oyster mushrooms
3¾ cups well flavored
vegetable stock (page 12)
salt and pepper
1 tablespoon chopped parsley

• Heat the oil and half the butter in a deep frying pan or heavy saucepan. Add the onion and cook over a low heat until transparent but not brown.
• Add the dry risotto rice to the pan and stir, coating it in the remaining fat. Mix with the onion. Fry over a medium heat, turning all the time for about 2 minutes.
• Pour half the stock into the pan and mix from the bottom up with a wooden spoon. Stir all the time, turning the rice grains over until the stock is absorbed. Add 1 teaspoon salt to the remaining stock and continue stirring until all the stock is absorbed. After 25 minutes the risotto should be of a creamy consistency without being too soft.
• Gently fry the mushroom slices and the halved oyster mushrooms in the remaining butter. Serve with the risotto, sprinkled with Parmesan cheese.
    A little saffron can be added with the stock for color and flavor.

Preparation Time: 10 minutes.
Cooking Time: 35 minutes.

Variation
Risotto Milanese
Substitute 1 cup white wine for an equal amount of vegetable stock and add to the rice as described above. Before serving, stir in 2 tablespoons butter and 2-3 tablespoons grated Parmesan cheese.

Stuffed Peppers

Serves 4

4 peppers, halved lengthways and deseeded
1 cup cooked rice, brown, white or a mixture
of both
2 tablespoons oil
1 onion, diced
2 cloves garlic, crushed
2 cups mushrooms, finely chopped
1 cup crushed tomatoes
Salt and pepper
1 teaspoon mushroom ketchup (optional)

- Place the halved peppers in a pan of boiling water and blanch for 2 minutes on a high heat. Drain and dry with kitchen paper. Cut 2 strips from each pepper for decoration.
- Arrange on an oiled baking sheet. Preheat the oven to 350ºF.
- Heat the oil and gently cook the onions and garlic over a low heat for about 5 minutes. Add the mushrooms and continue cooking for 5 minutes.
- Tip the onions and mushrooms into a bowl with the rice. Add the tomatoes, salt, pepper and mushroom ketchup. Mix well together with a wooden spoon.
- Divide the mixture among the 8 pepper halves. Decorate each one with 2 strips of pepper arranged in a cross.
- Paint with oil and cook in the oven for 15-20 minutes until piping hot.

Preparation Time: 15 minutes.
Cooking Time: 45 minutes.

OPPOSITE: *Vegetable Biriani (TOP)*
BELOW: *Stuffed Peppers*

Vegetable Biriani

Serves 4

*1 sweet red pepper, deseeded and cut
into strips*
2 onions
1 red chili, deseeded and cut into thin strips
3 zucchini, cut into slices
2 tablespoons lemon juice
1 tablespoon mild curry powder
1 cinnamon stick
1 teaspoon salt
1 cup yogurt
2 tablespoons oil
1¼ cups long-grain rice
¼ teaspoon saffron
8 whole cloves, 8 bay leaves
12 black peppercorns
½ teaspoon ground cinnamon
½ teaspoon ground cardamon
¼ cup butter
2 tablespoons raisins
½ cup cashew nuts

- Prepare the vegetables, arrange in the bottom of an ovenproof casserole and sprinkle with lemon juice.
- Mix the curry powder with the yogurt and spread over the vegetables, mixing well. Add the cinnamon stick and allow to stand for 1-2 hours.
- Preheat the oven to 350°F.
- Dice the onions finely or cut into very thin rings. Heat the oil and fry over a low heat for about 8 minutes. Take half the onions and mash or liquidize them and stir into the vegetables.
- Put the rice and spices into a pan of boiling salted water and cook at a rolling boil for 5 minutes. Drain, discarding the whole spices.
- Mix the remaining onion into the rice and lay on top of the vegetables. Cover tightly with a lid or foil and cook in the oven for 1 hour. Turn out onto a heated serving dish and mix the ingredients lightly with a fork. The rice should be fluffy. Lightly mix in the raisins and cashew nuts and garnish with a cinnamon stick.

Preparation Time: 25 minutes plus 2 hours standing time.
Cooking Time: 1 hour 5 minutes.

Fried Rice

Serves 4

3 tablespoons oil
1 onion, finely diced
2 cups cooked long-grain rice
Salt and pepper
½ cup frozen peas, thawed
1 cup bamboo shoots

- Heat the oil in a large pan or wok and toss the onion into the pan. Stir-fry for a few minutes, then add the rice.
- Season with salt and pepper and when the rice is hot, mix in the peas and bamboo shoots.
- Serve hot with other stir-fried vegetables or allow to cool and serve cold.

Preparation Time: 10 minutes.
Cooking Time: 30 minutes including time for cooking rice.

Variation
Fried rice can be served as a main course if made more substantial by adding other vegetables. Any of the following would be delicious: 1 cup mushrooms, sliced or button; 2 carrots, thinly sliced; sweet red, green or yellow peppers, deseeded and cut into strips; celery cut into sticks; green beans or snow peas. Stir-fry the vegetables until crisp and then add to the rice.

Breads

When time permits, making your own bread is one of the most satisfying of human activities. Yeastless speciality breads, such as the chapattis which accompany Indian food and Mexican tortillas, are all very simple to make and are ideal companions to a variety of vegetarian dishes.

The pizza was the invention of Neopolitan bakers as a cheap food for the poor of the city and bread dough spread with tomato and cheese is still a cheap dish which, though sometimes over-embellished with inappropriate additions, is popular world-wide.

A pizza is the perfect vehicle for fresh vegetables and a firm favorite with adults and children alike. Making your own is economical as well as allowing different members of the family to choose the toppings they prefer.

Basic pizzas freeze well and can have extra toppings added when they come out of the freezer and before baking.

Pizza Dough

Makes 2 x 10- to 12-inch thin-crust pizzas
Or 1 x10-inch deep-pan or rectangular pizza

2 cups all-purpose flour
$^1/_2$ teaspoon salt
2 teaspoons active dried yeast
1 teaspoon sugar, 1 tablespoon olive oil
$^3/_4$ cup slightly warmed milk
or a mixture of milk and water

- Sift the flour into a slightly warmed bowl with the salt. Sprinkle in the yeast and sugar and mix. Make a well in the center of the flour.

- Pour the oil into the milk and stir into the flour with a wooden spoon until a soft elastic dough forms.
- Knead on a floured board for about 5 minutes until soft and elastic to the touch (a mixer with a dough hook or a food processor with a plastic blade can be used).
- Put the dough in a lightly oiled plastic bag or into an oiled bowl covered with plastic film. Leave in a warm place (not too hot) until the dough doubles in size. This will take 30-45 minutes depending on the temperature.
- Turn out the dough onto a floured board and knead for at least 1 minutes to knock back the air bubbles.
- Roll out or knead into the shape of pizza required and fill as you wish.

Preparation Time: 1 hour

Variation
Wholewheat bread dough (page 92) and scone mix dough can also be used as pizza bases.

Quick Scone Pizza

1 pound all-purpose flour
2 teaspoons baking powder
1 teaspoon salt
$^1/_2$ cup butter or margarine
$1^1/_4$ cups milk

- Sift the flour, baking powder and salt into a bowl and rub in the fat until the mixture resembles fine breadcrumbs.
- Add the milk and mix to a soft dough. Roll out and shape into rounds. Place on an oiled baking sheet, arranging on it the pizza filling of your choice.

A long Italian or French loaf is ideal for a quick snack pizza. Cut in half, paint with olive oil and arrange tomato, cheese and any other topping you prefer. Bake in a hot oven for 6-8 minutes or place under the broiler.

Pissaladière

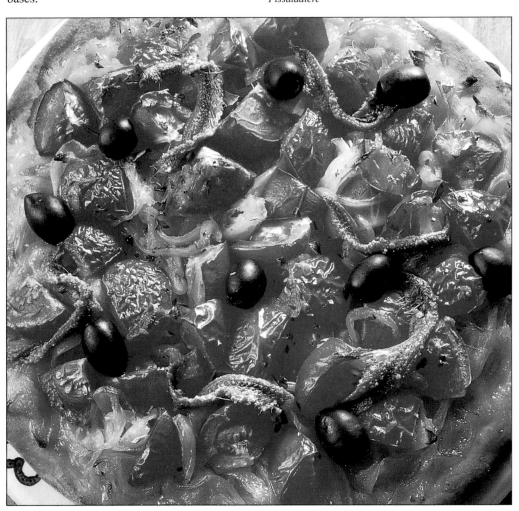

ABOVE: *Green Olive & Red Pepper Pizza* (page 90)

Pizza Margarita

Makes 2 x 10- to 12-inch pizzas
1 recipe Pizza Dough (see opposite)
1 tablespoon olive oil
$^{1}/_{4}$ recipe Tomato Sauce (page 36)
8 ounces Mozzarella cheese, grated or chopped
For the topping
8 ripe tomatoes, skinned and sliced
6 ounces Mozzarella cheese, thinly sliced
6 basil leaves, chopped
Freshly ground black pepper

• Preheat the oven to 425°F.
• Divide the dough into two pizzas and brush with olive oil. Spread half the tomato sauce on each. Sprinkle each with half the Mozzarella. Bake in a hot oven for 6-7 minutes.
• Meanwhile prepare the topping. Remove the pizzas from the oven and arrange slices of tomatoes and cheese alternately. Cover with basil and sprinkle with pepper. Drizzle on the remaining olive oil. Bake for a further 8 minutes.

Preparation Time: 1 hour.
Cooking Time: 16 minutes.

Pissaladière

Serves 4
$^{1}/_{2}$ recipe Pizza Dough (see opposite)
1 cup Tomato Sauce (page 36)
1 pound onions, after peeling
Salt and pepper, Black olives, pitted
6 large ripe tomatoes
1 tablespoon olive oil, Anchovies (optional)

• Make the dough and leave to prove while preparing the tomato sauce. Brush a 12-inch baking tin with oil.
• Slice the onions thinly and sauté them gently in olive oil until transparent but not browned. Drain and mix with the tomato sauce.
• Preheat the oven to 425°F.
• Roll out the dough and line the baking tin with it. Arrange the onion mixture on top and season.
• Cut the tomatoes into quarters and lay on top of the onions. Decorate with anchovies and black olives. Bake in the oven for about 20 minutes.

Preparation Time: 1 hour.
Cooking Time: 30 minutes.

Variation
Rich Pie Pastry (page 94), baked blind, can be used as an alternative base for the filling.

Neopolitan Pizza

Makes 2 x 10- to 12-inch pizzas
1 recipe Pizza Dough (page 88)
1 tablespoon olive oil
2 cloves garlic, crushed
1 cup crushed tomatoes
8 ripe tomatoes,
skinned and sliced
1 tablespoon chopped basil leaves
1 teaspoon oregano

• Preheat the oven to 220°F. Rub over 2 pizza rings or the bases of 2 flan rings with oil.

• Line with the pizza dough and brush over with oil. Crush the garlic and mix with the crushed tomatoes. Spread over the bases of the pizzas.

• Arrange the sliced tomatoes on the top, sprinkle with basil and oregano and sprinkle with the remaining oil. Bake in the oven for 15-20 minutes.

Preparation Time: 1 hour.
Cooking Time: 20 minutes.

Variation
Sun-dried tomatoes, sliced Mozzarella, olives, mushrooms, strips of pepper and onion rings can all be added to the topping.

Green Olive & Red Pepper Pizza

Makes 1 x 12-inch pizza
¹/₂ recipe Pizza Dough (page 88)
1 tablespoon olive oil
For the topping
1 large sweet red pepper, deseeded
2 tablespoons crushed tomatoes
1-2 cloves garlic, crushed
4 large ripe tomatoes, skinned and sliced
4 ounces Mozzarella cheese, grated
¹/₂ teaspoon dried oregano
Stuffed green olives, sliced

• Roll the dough into a rectangle and line a large baking tin. Brush over with olive oil.

• Preheat the oven to 425°F.

• Cut the pepper into rings and blanch in boiling water for 4 minutes. Drain well and dry on kitchen paper.

• Mix the garlic with the crushed tomatoes and spread over the base of the dough. Arrange the sliced tomatoes over the tomato mixture. Sprinkle with the Mozzarella cheese.

• Snip the pepper rings to make long strips. Arrange these in diamond shapes across the pizza and place the olives in the center of the diamonds. Bake for 20 minutes.

Preparation Time: 1 hour including rising time for dough.
Cooking Time: 20 minutes.

Variation
Half a recipe of Grilled Italian Vegetables (page 44) can be arranged on the pizza base which has been first covered with 1 cup Tomato Sauce (page 36). Top with grated Mozzarella cheese.

Neopolitan Pizza

Soft Tortillas

Spicy Vegetable Calzone

Serves 2

1 recipe Pizza Dough (page 88)
2 tablespoons oil
1 medium onion, finely chopped
2 garlic cloves, crushed
1 sweet red pepper, deseeded and diced
1 green chili pepper, deseeded and diced (optional)
1 cooked potato, diced
4 tomatoes, skinned and chopped
1 tablespoon tomato paste
2-3 drops chili sauce
4 tablespoon canned corn
Salt and pepper, 1 teaspoon dried oregano
4 ounces Mozzarella cheese, cut into cubes
1 beaten egg

- Make up the pizza dough and leave to rise while the vegetables are prepared.
- Heat the oil in a large frying pan and cook the onion and garlic over a gentle heat for about 4-5 minutes until transparent. Add the pepper, chili and potato and cook for another 2-3 minutes.
- Add the tomatoes, paste, chili sauce and canned corn. Mix well over the heat, season with salt and pepper and sprinkle with oregano. Turn onto a plate to cool.
- Preheat the oven to 220°F. Rub oil over a baking sheet.
- Divide the dough in 2 pieces and form each into 12-inch rounds (the loose bottom of a cake tin makes a good pattern). Divide the filling between the two rounds keeping it to one half of the circles. Add the cheese and brush the edges with egg. Fold over to make a half-moon shape, brush with egg, seal and bake for 15 minutes until golden brown.

Preparation Time: 1 hour.
Cooking Time: 15 minutes.

Variation
Use any favorite vegetable combinations such as eggplants, zucchini, sweet potatoes, carrots, peas and green beans.

Soft Tortillas

Makes 8

2 cups wholewheat flour
1 teaspoon baking powder, 1 teaspoon salt
$^1/_4$ cup vegetable cooking fat
4 tablespoons water

- Sift the flour, baking powder and salt into a bowl. Cut the fat into small lumps and rub roughly into the mixture.
- Add 3 tablespoons water and mix to a soft dough, adding remaining water if needed. Turn on to a floured board and knead the dough until smooth.
- Divide into 8 balls and cover with a clean cloth or plastic film and allow to stand for 15 minutes.
- Roll out each ball into a round large enough to cover a 6-inch plate. Oil a non-stick frying pan with some kitchen paper and place on medium heat for a few minutes. Cook the tortillas on both sides until golden brown and keep warm until required.
- Alternatively, store in the refrigerator or freezer in aluminum foil and reheat in the oven for a few minutes. Do not overcook or the tortillas will become hard.

Preparation Time: 25 minutes.
Cooking Time: 1 minute each side.

Variation
Use plain white flour for a lighter tortilla.

Chapattis

Makes 8
1¹/₂ cups wholewheat flour
¹/₄ teaspoon salt
³/₄ cup water

- Sprinkle the flour into a bowl with the salt and add the water gradually, mixing with a palette knife or spatula. Do not allow the dough to become sticky.
- Turn onto a floured board and knead until smooth. Cover the dough with a clean damp cloth and allow to stand for 30 minutes.
- Flour the board, knead the dough for 1 minute and form into a roll. Cut into 8 pieces.
- With floured hands, work each piece of dough into a ball. Roll or shape into 6-inch rounds and shake off excess flour. Heat a lightly oiled griddle or frying pan and fry on each side on a high heat: white spots will start to appear on the chapattis. Traditionally, each chapatti is put over a flame for a few seconds to puff up. This is more easily done under a broiler heated to maximum.
- Serve immediately or store wrapped in foil in the refrigerator. To reheat, place in a hot oven for 10 minutes. Serve with spicy dishes and curries.

Preparation Time: 40 minutes.
Cooking Time: 20 minutes.

Puris

Makes 12
1 cup wholewheat flour
1 cup all-purpose flour, sifted
¹/₂ teaspoon salt
2 tablespoons vegetable oil
¹/₂ cup water, oil for frying

- Tip the 2 flours into a bowl with the salt and 2 tablespoons vegetable oil. Rub in the oil until the mixture begins to take on a coarse, crumb-like texture. Add the water to form a stiff ball. Knead for about 10 minutes until smooth.
- Place in an oiled plastic bag and allow to stand for 30 minutes.
- Divide the mixture into 12 and keep covered with plastic film. Roll the balls out into 5-inch rounds. Cover each round with plastic film as you go.
- Heat about an inch of oil in a frying pan until very hot. Drop in the puris, one at a time, and press into the oil until they puff up. Turn over and repeat on other side. Drain on kitchen paper and keep warm until ready to serve.

Preparation Time: 40 minutes.
Cooking Time: 20 minutes.

Wholewheat Bread

Makes 2 x 8-inch round loaves
or 1 x 2-pound loaf or 2 x 1-pound loaves.
7¹/₂ cups wholewheat flour
2oz bran, 2 teaspoons salt
2 tablespoons white vegetable fat
1 pack active dry yeast
2¹/₂ cups warm water

- Mix the flour, bran and salt in a bowl. Rub in the fat and mix in the yeast. Prepare the water, making sure it is just warm (blood heat).
- Make a well in the center of the flour and add the water gradually, mixing the dough to incorporate all the flour. Do not add all the water at once.
- Turn onto a floured board and knead for 5-10 minutes or until the dough is of a soft elastic consistency. This can also be done in a food mixer with a dough hook or a food processor with a plastic blade.
- Place in an oiled plastic bag in a warm place until the dough has doubled in size. Knock back the dough and knead for 2 minutes, then cut into required pieces. To fill loaf tins, shape the pieces into rectangles, rolling them into cylinder shapes. Round loaves should have slightly domed tops.
- Allow to rise in the tins for about 1 hour or until the dough comes to the top of the tin.
- Preheat the oven to 230°F.
- Brush over with water and sprinkle with bran. Cook in the oven for about 40 minutes or until the loaf sounds hollow when tapped. Leave in the tin for 5 minutes, then turn out on to a wire cooling rack.

Preparation Time: 2 hours with rising time.
Cooking Time: 40 minutes.

RIGHT: *Chapattis, Puris*

Pastry

Pastry consists of a mixture of flour, fat and water, sometimes with additions, and the different types are simply variations on this theme. The same basic ingredients are always used but in different proportions and with various cooking temperatures as well as methods of preparation. How you handle pastry greatly contributes to its success or failure:

Handle lightly • Work quickly • Keep pastry cool

When handling pastry it is a good idea to run the wrists under cold water to cool the hands and to use a marble rolling pin and pastry board if at all possible. Set aside a special time to make pastry before other cooking makes the temperature in the kitchen too high.

Fortunately, there are available many excellent brands of prepared pastry for cooks disinclined to make their own or who just do not have sufficient time. It is useful to keep frozen puff pastry, phyllo and pie pastry in the freezer when a single- or double-crust pie, flan or turnover will be simple and easy to produce. To make life even easier, partially cooked pastries or the unbaked pie shells available in stores and supermarkets can also be used. These can be filled with fresh or frozen vegetables, sliced fruits and even quiche mixtures – all guaranteed to add variety to the vegetarian diet.

shape until it is smaller than the plate.
- Lift the pastry into the plate, unfold and ease it in without stretching the pastry. Trim and remove the trimmings.
- Preheat the oven to 400°F.

Preparation Time: 10 minutes.

Blind baking a pastry shell
Prick the base of the shell. Line with greaseproof paper and cover with dried or ceramic beans. This will prevent the pastry rising. Cook for 20 minutes, then take from the oven and remove the beans with the paper. Return to the oven to crisp for 5-6 minutes.

Pie weights
Dried kidney beans, navy beans, rice, pasta or even bread crusts placed on a paper lining can all be used. However, these have limited storage life and can begin to smell unsavory after being used a few times. For keen cooks interested in making pies and flans regularly, it is advisable to buy metal or ceramic pie weights from a kitchen shop. These can be washed, dried and stored ready for the next time and will last indefinitely.

Do not prick the pastry if the filling is to be cooked inside the raw pastry case.

Pie Pastry

Makes 10- to 12-inch pastry shells or
8 ounces pastry
2 cups all-purpose flour
1/2 teaspoon salt
1 cup butter
or hard margarine
Cold water

- Sift the flour and salt into a medium-sized bowl and cut the fat into pieces. Add the fat to the flour and rub in with the tips of the fingers or with a pastry blender until the mixture resembles fine breadcrumbs. Allow as much air as possible to get into the mixture and shake the bowl from time to time when any lumps will come to the surface and can be disposed of.
- Gradually add a little of the water, using a palette knife or plastic spatula to mix. When

the mixture begins to form into a ball, mix well with clean hands, adding more water a drop at a time if the mixture appears to be too dry and crumbly. Work the ball of pastry lightly until smooth. Wrap in plastic film or foil and allow to rest in the refrigerator for at least 20 minutes. Roll out on a floured board and use as required.

Preparation Time: 10 minutes, plus 20 minutes resting time.

To line a pie plate with pastry
Roll the pastry on a floured board with a lightly floured rolling pin in short sharp strokes away from you. Move the pastry around with a quarter turn each time to prevent sticking and to produce a round shape. Do not turn the pastry over.
- Roll the pastry out to a circle extending 1 1/2 inches beyond an ungreased pie plate. Fold the circle inwards into a five-sided

Rich Pie Pastry

To line 2 x 6- to 7-inch flan rings
or pie plates
or 1 x 12-inch plate
2 cups all-purpose flour
1/4 teaspoon salt
3/4 cup butter, hard margarine
or white vegetable fat
1 egg yolk
1-2 tablespoon cold water

- Sift the flour and salt into a bowl and cut the fat into chunks. Rub into the mixture until it resembles fine breadcrumbs. Mix the egg yolk and water together in a small dish and add to the bowl, stirring in with a fork until the mixture is soft but not sticky. If too stiff, add a few drops of cold water very gradually.
- Turn out onto a floured board and knead

Mediterranean Quiche (page 96)

lightly. Wrap in plastic film and rest in the refrigerator for at least 20 minutes.

Preparation Time: 10 minutes plus chilling time.

Variations

Cheese Pastry

Sift $\frac{1}{4}$ teaspoon dried mustard and paprika into the flour and salt. Use only $\frac{1}{2}$ cup butter and, after this is rubbed into the flour mixture, stir in $\frac{3}{4}$ cup strong grated cheese. Continue as for Rich Pie Pastry.

Sweet Pie Pastry

Prepare as above but mix in 2 tablespoons superfine sugar before adding the egg. Use for fruit pies.

Wholewheat Pastry

Use 2 cups wholewheat flour (or half wholewheat and half white) with $\frac{1}{2}$ cup butter, or half hard margarine or white vegetable fat. Mix with 7-8 tablespoons cold water and a few drops of oil.

Mushroom Quiche

Make 8 ounces unsweetened pastry using any
of the recipes on pages 94-95

Serves 2-4
1 x 8-inch baked pastry shell
2 eggs
Salt and pepper
4 tablespoons cream
2 tablespoons butter
3-4 scallions, sliced
1 cup mushrooms, sliced
1 tablespoon grated cheese
(optional)

• Preheat the oven to 400°F.
• Break the eggs into a bowl and add
  seasoning and the cream. Beat together
  using a fork or a whisk until well mixed.
• Melt the butter in a small pan and gently
  cook the scallions and mushrooms for
  a few minutes over a medium heat.
  Remove from the pan and allow to cool.
  Reduce the oven temperature to 350ºF.
• Arrange the mushrooms and onions in the
  pastry shell, pour over the egg mixture and
  cook in the oven for about 20 minutes or

until golden brown. Add cheese before
baking, if liked.

Preparation Time: 25 minutes plus 20 minutes
resting time for pastry.
Cooking Time: 30 minutes.

Variations

Onion Quiche

Slice 1 pound onions thinly. Heat $\frac{1}{4}$ cup
butter in a frying pan and add the onions. Stir
over a medium heat for at least 5 minutes,
making sure the onions do not brown. Allow
to cool.

Place in the pastry shell and pour in the
egg and cream mixture. Sprinkle with finely
chopped parsley. Cook in the preheated oven
(see Mushroom Quiche) until golden brown
for about 25 minutes.

8 ounces pastry will make 6 x 3-inch
individual shells.

Spinach Quiche

Cook or steam a generous 1 pound washed
spinach without stalks for about 5-7
minutes. Drain well and arrange in the pastry
shell. Cover with egg and cream. If liked,
sprinkle with 2 tablespoons grated cheese
before baking.

Spinach & Lentil Quiche

Prepare the spinach as for Spinach Quiche
and allow to cool. Chop 2 medium onions
finely. Heat 2 tablespoons vegetable oil in a
heavy saucepan and cook the onions gently
over a low heat for about 5 minutes or until
they are transparent. Add $\frac{1}{2}$ cup washed red
lentils and stir well before adding $1\frac{1}{2}$ cups
water, $\frac{1}{2}$ teaspoon ground coriander and $\frac{1}{2}$
teaspoon cumin. Simmer until the lentils are
almost a purée. Cool slightly and mix with
the spinach, 2 teaspoons lemon juice, salt and
pepper.

Pour into the pastry shell and cover with
a piece of aluminum foil before cooking for
25 minutes.

Leek Quiche

Wash, thoroughly dry and slice 2 leeks. Heat
$\frac{1}{4}$ cup butter in a pan and cook the leeks
gently over a low heat for about 5 minutes.
Cool and arrange in the bottom of the pastry
shell. Add the egg and cream mixture. Top
with skinned sliced tomato before baking, if
liked.

Mediterranean Quiche

Remove the skins from 4 large tomatoes
and cut into slices. Slice an onion and cook
for about 4 minutes in 1 tablespoon olive oil.
Allow to cool. Arrange the tomato and onion
in the pastry shell, sprinkling with 4-6
chopped basil leaves and chopped black
olives. Add the egg and cream and bake.

Onion Quiche

Wholewheat Pastry Cushions

Serves 4 as a main course
For the Pastry
2 cups wholewheat flour
1 teaspoon salt, $^1/_2$ cup sunflower oil
A little cold water
For the Filling
2 medium potatoes, cooked and diced
1 carrot, diced and cooked
3 tablespoons sunflower oil
1 onion, finely chopped
1 small piece peeled ginger, finely chopped
1 clove garlic, crushed
$^1/_2$ teaspoon turmeric
$^1/_2$ teaspoon chili powder
$^1/_2$ teaspoon garam masala
2 tomatoes, peeled and diced
$^1/_2$ cup frozen peas, thawed
2 tablespoons fresh coriander, chopped

- Put the flour and salt into a bowl. Add the oil and work with the finger tips or a pastry blender until the mixture resembles coarse breadcrumbs. Add the water gradually and mix to a fairly firm consistency. Turn out onto a lightly floured board and roll into a ball. Cover with plastic film and leave to rest for 30 minutes

- Heat the oil and add the onion over a low heat. Allow to cook until transparent. Add the ginger, garlic and spices and stir well. Gently stir in the potatoes, carrots and peas with the chopped tomato.

- Add 4 tablespoons water and allow to simmer for about 10 minutes, then sprinkle with coriander and allow to cool.

- Turn out the pastry onto a lightly floured board and roll it out, cutting it into 3- x 2-inch strips. Brush round the edges with cold water and place a spoonful of filling in the center of one half of each strip.

- Fold over to make rectangles and seal the edges. Heat oil in a deep pan to 375°F and fry the cushions in batches of three. Drain on kitchen paper and serve with Tzatziki (page 25) or Mint & Yogurt Dip (page 24).

Preparation Time: 25 minutes plus resting time for pastry.
Cooking Time: 25 minutes.

Variation
Cook in the oven at 400°F for 10-15 minutes or, if preferred, deep fry in oil.

Broccoli & Asparagus Roll

Serves 6
8 ounces phyllo pastry
$1^1/_4$ pounds broccoli florets, trimmed
6 asparagus spears, fresh or canned
2 hard-boiled eggs
1 cup brown or white rice, cooked
$^1/_4$ teaspoon nutmeg
Salt and pepper
1-2 tablespoon heavy cream
2 tablespoons butter, melted
2 tablespoons pine nuts
1 teaspoon sesame seeds
$1^1/_4$ cups Hollandaise (page 37) or Tomato Sauce (page 36)

Broccoli & Asparagus Roll

- Cook the broccoli for 8 minutes and drain well. Cook the asparagus for 10 minutes, if using fresh. Chop or sieve the eggs into a bowl with the rice, season and sprinkle with nutmeg. Add the cream, broccoli, asparagus (cut into pieces) and pine nuts and mix roughly. Preheat the oven to 350°F.

- Arrange layers of the phyllo pastry in a sheet measuring 12 x 10 inches. Spread the broccoli and asparagus mixture down the center. Brush the edges of the pastry with melted butter and roll up, tucking in the ends. Place seam side down on a baking tray and brush with more melted butter.Sprinkle on the sesame seeds.

- Cook in a moderate oven until golden brown, about 35 minutes. Serve with new potatoes and Hollandaise or tomato sauce.

Preparation Time: 15 minutes.
Cooking Time: 45 minutes.

Variation
Puff pastry can be used in very much the same way as phyllo, but cook at 450F. for about 35 minutes.

Mixed Vegetable Pie

Serves 4-6

8 ounces frozen puff pastry, thawed
2 tablespoons oil
2 onions, finely diced
3 carrots, thinly sliced
4 potatoes, cooked and sliced
$^1/_2$ cup fresh or frozen peas
$^3/_4$ cup grated cheese
Salt and pepper

- Heat the oil in a pan and allow the onions to cook over a low heat without browning for about 4 minutes. Add the carrots and allow the two vegetables to cook gently for a further 5 minutes.

- Meanwhile, cook the peas and drain well. Allow all the ingredients to cool down for 15 minutes.
- Preheat the oven to 400°F.
- Roll out the pastry and use half to line a deep 9-inch pie plate, allowing a small amount to overhang the edge of the dish. Arrange a layer of onions, carrots and peas on the bottom of the pastry. Sprinkle with salt and pepper and some grated cheese.
- Arrange a layer of sliced cooked potato and sprinkle with cheese and seasoning. Continue with the the remaining ingredients in layers until all the ingredients have been used.
- Roll out a round of pastry larger than the circumference of the dish. Wet the edge of the pie dish with water and cover with the pastry lid. Without stretching the pastry,

seal the edges and trim through both layers with a sharp knife. Use the left-over pastry scraps to make leaves to decorate the pie. Brush with egg to add shine and a golden color to the finished pie (optional) and bake in the oven for 30 minutes.

Preparation Time: 30 minutes plus resting time for pastry.
Cooking Time:1 hour.

Mixed Vegetable Pie

Leek Pie

Serves 4-6

3 cups Béchamel Sauce (page 35)
¼ cup butter or margarine
2¼ pounds leeks, sliced
1 onion, sliced
2 cups cooked rice
4 tomatoes, skinned
7 ounces corn, drained
1 tablespoon chopped chives
2 hard-boiled eggs (optional)
Salt and pepper
8-ounce pack frozen puff pastry, thawed

• Prepare the sauce and keep until required, covered with plastic film to avoid a skin forming.

• Melt the butter over a medium heat in a large frying pan and add the onion. Turn down the heat and allow to cook for about 3 minutes, then add the leeks gradually, stirring into the butter and onion. Cook gently for about 5 minutes without browning the vegetables.

• Arrange a layer of leeks in the bottom of an oval pie dish and cover with some of the sauce. Next add a layer of rice and season well.

• Add the corn and then some sauce and more rice on top.

• Cut the tomatoes in slices and arrange on top of the corn.

• Start again with the leeks and finish up the vegetables. If using eggs, slice and layer near the top.

• Preheat the oven to 450°F.

• Roll out the pastry into an oval shape slightly larger than the pie dish. Cut round the oval to produce a piece of pastry for the lip of the dish. Wet the rim and place pastry firmly onto the rim.

• Brush rim pastry with cold water and place the large oval of pastry onto the pie. Trim pastry to fit the dish, knock up the edges and flute. Make slits for the steam to escape.

• Make some shapes to decorate the top, brush with beaten egg and cook in the oven for 30 minutes or until golden brown. Serve with potatoes and a crisp green vegetable.

Preparation Time: 30 minutes.
Cooking Time: 1 hour.

Leek Pie

Tasty Pasties

Serves 4

For the pastry

2 cups wholewheat flour

4 tablespoons each of oil and water

$\frac{1}{2}$ teaspoon salt

For the filling

$\frac{1}{4}$ cup brown lentils

1 large potato, boiled then peeled

2 tablespoons oil, 1 onion, diced

2 carrots, scraped and diced

1 sweet red or green pepper,
deseeded and diced

1 zucchini, diced

$\frac{1}{2}$ teaspoon mixed dried herbs or 1
tablespoon fresh

1 teaspoon lemon juice

$\frac{1}{2}$ teaspoon curry powder

1 tablespoon mango chutney

7-ounce can plum tomatoes, drained
(but retain juice)

- Prepare the pastry (pages 94-95), substituting the oil for butter or margarine, and leave to rest in the refrigerator. Boil the potato until tender but still firm and dice when cool. Cook the lentils until soft.
- Heat the oil in a pan and cook the onion over a low heat for about 4 minutes without browning. Add the carrots, pepper and zucchini. Cook for a further 3 minutes.
- Add the lemon juice, curry powder and the tomatoes, chopped. Mix well and stir in 4 tablespoons tomato juice. Season and simmer for 20 minutes until the vegetables are tender.
- Stir in the lentils, potatoes and mango chutney, remove from the heat and tip into a clean bowl to cool.
- Roll out the pastry and divide into two. Roll out one half and cut out 2 rounds of 6-7 inches. Brush round the edges with water, and put one quarter of the filling in each. Turn over and finish the edges with a fork or flute with the fingers. Make three small

slits on the top and place on a baking sheet.
- Repeat with the other half of the pastry.
- Deep fry the pasties in very hot oil until brown and puffed up, cooking no more than two at a time. Remove and drain on kitchen paper.

Preparation Time: 30 minutes plus resting time for pastry.
Cooking Time: 1 hour.

Variation

Use leeks, mushrooms and any other favorite vegetable to ring the changes. Use rice in place of lentils or more potato. These pasties make excellent packed lunches or picnics accompanied by a mixed salad.

Miniature Tasty Pasties

These are good for snacks and buffet parties. Make up 1 pound of pastry. Divide the pastry in two and roll both halves into squares. Fill and cut into 2-inch squares.

Phyllo Pastry Parcels

Serves 4

1 tablespoon oil
2 tablespoons butter or margarine
6 scallions, finely sliced
3 cups mushrooms, thinly sliced
Salt and pepper
$\frac{1}{4}$ teaspoon nutmeg
4 tomatoes, skinned and sliced
2 eggs, hard-boiled, sliced
4 tablespoon low fat cream cheese
8-ounce pack phyllo pastry

• Heat the oil and butter and add the scallions and mushrooms. Cook over a medium heat for about 4 minutes. Add seasonings and allow to cool.
• Preheat the oven to 400°F.
• Separate the layers of phyllo and cover to prevent them from drying out while making up the parcels.
• Arrange the pastry in layers crossing each other to make a square 8 x 8 inches. Divide into 4 pieces. Put a quarter of the onion/mushroom mixture on the bottom of each piece, season with pepper and cover with 1 tablespoon cream cheese. Divide a quarter of the tomatoes and eggs in layers between the squares.
• Wet the edges of the parcels and tuck the pastry in as if tying a paper parcel. If liked, brush with egg and milk.
• Cook in the oven for about 20 minutes until the pastry is golden. Serve immediately accompanied by crisp vegetables such zucchini or green beans and new potatoes.

Preparation Time: 30 minutes.
Cooking Time: 40 minutes.

OPPOSITE: *Miniature Tasty Pasties*
BELOW: *Phyllo Pastry Parcels*

Savory Rice Parcels

Serves 4

2 tablespoons vegetable oil
1 small onion, finely chopped
1 red pepper,
deseeded and cut into small dice
1 cup cooked rice, salt and pepper
2 scallions
2 tomatoes, skinned and diced
2 hard-boiled eggs, chopped
2 tablespoons sour cream
1 tablespoon chopped parsley
8-ounce pack phyllo pastry

• Heat the oil in a frying pan and cook the onion and red pepper for about 6 minutes. Allow to cool then add the remaining ingredients, mix well and allow to cool. Prepare the pastry as in previous recipe, fill the squares with the mixture and bake.

Asparagus Galette

Serves 4

4 ounces puff pastry
8 ounces asparagus, trimmed
2 eggs
2 tablespoons heavy cream
Salt and pepper
1 ripe tomato
1 teaspoon chopped chives
1 teaspoon chopped basil
2 tablespoons Parmesan cheese, grated
For the garnish
Fresh basil leaves

- Preheat the oven to 425°F. Prepare a baking sheet by rinsing in cold water.
- Cook the asparagus until tender but still crisp, then drain well.
- Roll out the pastry to a circle about 9-10 inches across. Use the bottom of a loose-bottomed cake tin, if you have one, or draw a circle on a piece of paper. Roll out the pastry slightly beyond this circle and cut round it so that you are left with a narrow ring of pastry which will form the raised edge of the galette.
- Place the circle of pastry on the tray and prick with a fork. Brush the edge with cold water and lay the narrow strip of pastry around the edge. Cook in the oven for about 15 minutes. Remove and allow to cool slightly. Lower the oven to 325°F.
- Arrange the tomatoes on the pastry, then the asparagus spears.
- Beat up the egg with cream, seasoning and herbs. Carefully pour on top of the vegetables. Sprinkle with grated cheese and cook in the oven until set and the top is golden brown. Garnish with basil leaves.

Preparation Time: 30 minutes.
Cooking Time: 1 hour.

Asparagus Galette

Potato & Mushroom Pie

Serves 4

8 ounces Pie Pastry (page 94)
1 pound peeled potatoes, sliced
2 tablespoons oil
1-2 cloves garlic, crushed
1 large onion, cut into thin rings
12 ounces large mushrooms, sliced
1 cup light cream
2 tablespoons chopped parsley
3 tablespoons grated cheese
$1/4$ teaspoon cayenne pepper
Beaten egg to glaze pastry

- Make the pastry and put in the refrigerator to rest.
- Place the evenly-sliced potatoes in a pan of salted water and bring to the boil. Allow to boil for 3-4 minutes, then drain into a colander.
- Heat the oil in a large pan and over a low heat cook the garlic and onion rings for about 4 minutes, then add the mushrooms. Cook gently for another 5 minutes. Add the cream, parsley, grated cheese and cayenne pepper.
- Preheat the oven to 400°F.
- Place about one third of the potatoes in the bottom of a buttered 9-inch pie dish.
- Cover the potatoes with half the mushroom mixture and continue with half the remaining potatoes. Use the mushroom mixture to top the second layer of potatoes, finishing with potatoes.
- Roll out the pastry and cover the dish as described on page 94. Brush with egg and cook in the oven for 20 minutes, then reduce the temperature to 325°F and continue cooking for a further 30 minutes.

Preparation Time: 25 minutes.
Cooking Time: 1 hour.

Savory Choux Buns

Makes 6

$3/4$ cup all-purpose flour
$1/4$ teaspoon salt
1 cup water
2 tablespoons butter or margarine
2 eggs, beaten
For the filling
$1^1/4$ cups Mushroom Sauce (page 34)

- Preheat the oven to 400°F. Grease 2 baking sheets.
- Sift the flour and salt onto a plate or piece of aluminum foil.
- Heat the water and the fat over a gentle heat until the fat is dissolved then bring to the boil and tip in the flour.
- Beat with a wooden spoon until the dough is smooth. Continue cooking until the dough forms a ball and leaves the side of the pan. Remove from the heat (do not overbeat).
- When the sides of the pan have cooled, add the beaten egg a little at a time until it is well incorporated and has formed into a paste.
- Either pipe the mixture using a piping bag with a large nozzle or spoon onto the baking sheets, dividing the mixture evenly into 6. Bake in the oven for 30-35 minutes until golden brown and well puffed up.
- Remove from the oven and make a slit in the side of each bun to allow the steam to escape. Return to the oven for 6 minutes, then cool slightly on a wire tray.
- Fill with mushroom sauce and serve hot with a green salad.

Preparation Time: 20 minutes.
Cooking Time: 1 hour.

Variation
Vegetables with curry or other savory sauces can be used to fill choux pastry. Small buns make excellent starters or buffet finger food and can be used as profiteroles or filled with fruit and cream.

Salads

All kinds of vegetables and fruits, cooked and uncooked, can be used in salads. The simple addition of cooked pasta, rice, beans and lentils can transform a light salad into a complete and nutritious meal. Make good use of the entire spectrum of exotic vegetables and fruits available throughout the year to add color, texture and excitement to salad dishes.

Instant Shredded Salad

This salad takes only a few minutes to prepare in the food processor.

Serves 4-6
1 sweet red, 1 green and 1 yellow pepper
½ cucumber
2 carrots, scraped
¼ white cabbage, washed
½ iceberg lettuce, washed and dried

- Blanch the peppers in a pan of boiling water for 2 minutes, drain and cool under cold water. Remove the top and the seeds and cut in half.
- Using the finest blade on the food processor, slice all the vegetables including half the lettuce.
- Tear the remaining half lettuce and use it to line the salad bowl. Mix all the vegetables together with the dressing of your choice (page 38) or serve the dressing separately.

Preparation Time: 10 minutes.
Cooking Time: 2 minutes.

Green & Red Salad

Serves 6-8
1 Boston or bib lettuce
1 romaine lettuce
1 escarole lettuce
1 head radicchio
1 bunch watercress, thick stalks removed

- Wash the lettuces and drain thoroughly. Dry on kitchen paper or in a clean dish towel.
- Tear the larger leaves to a suitable size and arrange in a pretty salad bowl. Cover with plastic film and store in the refrigerator until required. Serve with any of the salad dressings on page 38.

  Do not add dressing to a leafy salad until just before serving or it will become soggy and inedible.

LEFT: *Instant Shredded Salad*

Caesar Salad

Serves 4
4 tablespoons olive oil
Juice of 1 lemon
1 clove garlic, crushed
Salt and pepper
1 Cos lettuce, washed and dried
1/2 cup Parmesan cheese, grated
2 hard-boiled eggs, sieved
For the croûtons
6 tablespoons vegetable oil
2 thick slices of bread,
cut into small dice

BELOW: *Waldorf Salad*

- Pour the oil, lemon juice, garlic and seasoning into a screw-top jar. Shake well and allow to stand for 30 minutes.
- Heat the oil for the croûtons in a large frying pan and fry the cubes of bread in hot oil for a few minutes until golden. Drain on kitchen paper.
- Arrange the lettuce and cheese in a salad bowl. Sprinkle in the dressing (strain if preferred) and mix the lettuce with the drained croûtons. Sieve the egg over the salad.

Preparation Time: 10 minutes plus standing time for dressing.
Cooking time: 10 minutes for eggs.

Cucumber Salad

Serves 4
1 medium cucumber, thinly sliced
1 teaspoon salt
1 tablespoon sugar
1 1/2 cups cider vinegar
Pepper
Chopped parsley or dill

- Sprinkle the slices of cucumber with salt. Leave to stand for 20 minutes. Remove the excess water from the cucumber with kitchen paper.
- Place the cucumber in a dish. Mix the sugar and vinegar together and pour over the cucumber. Sprinkle with pepper.
- Taste for seasoning and drain off the liquid. Arrange in a dish and sprinkle with the dill or the parsley. Serve immediately.

Waldorf Salad

Serves 4
1 head of celery, strings removed
2 red-skinned apples,
cored and cut into slices
2 tablespoons lemon juice
8 shelled walnuts,
roughly chopped
1/2 cup raisins or sultanas
1/2 cup seedless grapes, washed
4 tablespoons heavy cream
4 tablespoons Mayonnaise
(page 35)

- Chop the celery into thin slices and put into a salad bowl. Add the apple slices and pour over the lemon juice.
- Mix the walnuts, raisins and seedless grapes together with the cream and mayonnaise. Arrange this mixture on top of the celery and apples.
- Chill, then fold all the salad ingredients together just before serving.

Preparation Time: 15 minutes.

Variation
The bowl can be lined with crisp lettuce leaves and chopped pineapple (canned or fresh) can be added to the salad.

Pasta Salad Niçoise

Serves 4

8 ounces pasta twists, cooked and drained
4 scallions, chopped
8 ounces small green beans, cooked
but still crisp
$1/2$ cup Vinaigrette (page 38)
4 ripe tomatoes, skinned
Black olives, pitted

- Put the drained and cooled pasta into a bowl and mix well with the scallions and green beans. Pour on the vinaigrette and allow to stand for at least 10 minutes. Arrange in a serving dish.
- Cut the tomatoes into wedges and arrange on the pasta salad with the olives. Serve with a crisp green salad.

Preparation Time: 15 minutes.
Cooking Time: 18 minutes.

Quick Rice Salad

Serves 4

1 small can sweet red peppers, drained
and diced
2 cups cooked long-grain rice
4 scallions, finely chopped
1 cup canned corn
2 tablespoon chopped coriander
Juice and rind of $1/2$ lemon
$1/2$ cup Vinaigrette (page 38)

- Blanch the peppers in boiling water for 2 minutes, drain and cool.
- Mix all the ingredients together and serve in a suitable bowl.

Preparation Time: 10 minutes.
Cooking Time: 15 minutes for rice.

Tomatoes Vinaigrette

Serves 4

6 large ripe tomatoes,
skinned and thinly sliced
Salt and pepper
1 red onion, finely sliced
For the dressing
6 tablespoons olive oil
2 tablespoons white wine vinegar
$1/2$ teaspoon French mustard
Salt and pepper
$1/2$ teaspoon sugar
2 tablespoons fresh chives, chopped
1 tablespoon chopped parsley

- Arrange the tomatoes and onion slices on a flat dish.
- Place all the ingredients for the dressing in a screw-top jar, shake well and pour over the tomatoes.

Pasta Salad Niçoise

Green Pasta Salad

Turkish Cucumber Salad

Serves 4
1 large cucumber, diced
2 teaspoons sea salt, black pepper
4 cloves garlic, crushed
2 cups thick yogurt
4 tablespoons fresh mint, chopped

• Put the diced cucumber into a colander and sprinkle with salt. Allow to drain for 1 hour. Squeeze the cucumber with your hands and dry on kitchen paper.
• In the meantime mix the garlic with the yogurt, a good shake of pepper and the mint.
• Mix together just before serving.

Preparation Time: 10 minutes plus 1 hour draining time for cucumbers.

Green Pasta Salad

Serves 4
8 ounces spinach tortellini
4 ounces snow peas
1 crisp lettuce, washed
1 endive
6 tablespoons yogurt
2 tablespoons lemon juice
Salt and pepper

• Cook the tortellini in boiling salted water for about 8 minutes or until tender. Drain into a colander or sieve and run under cold water to cool.
• Cook the snow peas in a little boiling salted water for about 4 minutes, drain and run under the cold tap to cool. Separate the leaves from the endive and use them to line a serving dish. Arrange the lettuce leaves and the pasta on top.
• Mix the yogurt, lemon juice, salt and pepper together and pour over the artichokes.
• Arrange the snow peas and tortellini in the bowl and, just before serving, toss the salad lightly to mix.

Preparation Time: 10 minutes.
Cooking Time: 14 minutes.

Variation
Lightly cooked asparagus tips or artichoke hearts can also be used in the salad.

Marinated Mushrooms

Serves 4

2 cups button mushrooms, washed
1 cup dry white wine
2 tablespoons olive oil
Salt and pepper
$\frac{1}{2}$ teaspoon nutmeg
$\frac{1}{2}$ teaspoon fresh ginger, grated
2 tablespoons chopped fresh coriander
1 bay leaf

For the garnish
1 tomato, peeled
1 tablespoon chopped fresh thyme

- Trim the stalks of the mushrooms and put the stalks and caps in a bowl.
- Pour the wine and olive oil into a screw-top jar. Season with salt and pepper and add the nutmeg, ginger, coriander and the bay leaf.

Replace the lid and shake vigorously. Pour over the mushrooms and allow to stand covered for two hours.

- Cut the tomato into wedges. Arrange the mushrooms in a suitable dish and pour over the marinade. Garnish with the tomato wedges, a bay leaf and thyme.

Preparation Time: 10 minutes plus 2 hours marinating

Greek Salad

Serves 4

1 small crisp lettuce, washed and dried
2 large ripe tomatoes,
each cut into 8 wedges
$\frac{1}{4}$ cucumber, diced, 2 scallions, sliced
Juice of 1 lemon, Salt and pepper
4 ounces feta cheese, sliced
12 pitted black olives

- Tear the lettuce leaves and line a salad bowl. Add the tomatoes, cucumber and scallions.
- Sprinkle with lemon juice, salt and pepper.
- Arrange the feta cheese and black olives on the salad.

Preparation Time: 10 minutes

Coleslaw Deluxe

Serves 4

3 celery stalks, strings removed
2 carrots peeled and grated
1 small white cabbage, finely shredded
2 small sweet green peppers, deseeded
1 small onion, finely chopped
2 scallions, finely chopped
$\frac{1}{2}$ cup raisins (optional)

For the dressing
1 cup Mayonnaise (page 35)
1 tablespoon thin cream
1 tablespoon white wine vinegar
$\frac{1}{2}$ teaspoon salt
$\frac{1}{2}$ teaspoon sugar
$\frac{1}{4}$ teaspoon pepper
$\frac{1}{4}$ teaspoon paprika

- Put all the ingredients for the dressing into a large salad bowl and whisk thoroughly together.
- Cut the celery into $\frac{1}{4}$-inch slices and add them to the bowl with the carrot and cabbage. Mix well.
- Cut the peppers into thin strips and blanch in boiling water for 2 minutes. Drain and allow to cool.
- Add the onion, scallions, peppers and raisins. Mix well with the other ingredients and allow to stand covered in the refrigerator for 1 hour. Remove from the refrigerator 15 minutes before required and stir to mix the dressing thoroughly before serving.

Preparation Time: 30 minutes or 10 minutes if using the food processor plus standing time.

Marinated Mushrooms

Toasted Walnut & Roquefort Salad

Serves 4

1 cup shelled walnuts
4 ounces Roquefort cheese, crumbled
Salt and pepper
6 tablespoons vegetable oil
16 thin slices of French bread from a slim baguette
1 crisp lettuce, washed
2 bunches watercress,
washed and with stalks removed

For the dressing

3-4 tablespoons walnut oil
2 tablespoons safflower oil
2 teaspoons French mustard
Salt and pepper
$1/_4$ teaspoon sugar
2 tablespoons white wine vinegar

- Preheat the oven to 350°F.
- Retain 1 tablespoon walnut oil. Put the rest of the dressing ingredients into a screw-top jar and shake well.
- Place the walnuts in a bowl with the 1 tablespoon walnut oil and turn the nuts over until coated. Sprinkle with salt and pepper. Arrange on a baking tray and put into the oven to toast for about 10 minutes.
- Heat the vegetable oil in a large frying pan and fry the bread until golden on both sides. Drain on kitchen paper.
- Arrange 4 slices of bread on 4 warmed plates.
- Put the lettuce and cress in a bowl and pour over the dressing, mix well and divide onto the four plates.
- Top with warm walnuts and crumbled cheese.

Preparation Time: 20 minutes.
Cooking Time:15-20 minutes.

Red Cabbage & Apple Salad

Serves 4

1 pound red cabbage
3 dessert apples, cored
2 tablespoons lemon juice
1 red onion, cut into thin rings
$1/_4$ cup dry white wine
4 tablespoons oil
Salt and pepper
$1/_2$ teaspoon powdered ginger
1 cup light cream
1 tablespoon lemon juice

- Slice the red cabbage into thin wedges and place in a large pan of boiling salted water for 5 minutes. Drain in a colander and cool.
- Arrange the onions on the cabbage wedges in a salad bowl. Mix the wine and oil together with the seasoning and ginger in a screw-top jar. Shake vigorously and pour over the cabbage. Allow to stand in the refrigerator for 30 minutes.
- Cut the cored apples into quarters and then into slices and sprinkle with lemon juice.
- Mix the apples with the cabbage and onion. Add the cream just before serving.

Preparation Time: 10 minutes plus 30 minutes standing time.
Cooking Time: 5 minutes.

Red Cabbage & Apple Salad

Egg & Cress Salad

Serves 4

6 medium hard-boiled eggs
2 bunches watercress,
washed and drained
1 carton mustard and cress
12 radishes, thinly sliced
¼ cup Vinaigrette (page 38)

- Slice the eggs in quarters. Drain and dry the watercress and remove the thick stalks. Wash and dry the mustard and cress on kitchen paper.
- Divide the watercress in 5 bunches and arrange around a salad bowl. Position 2 egg quarters between the bunches and the remainder in the middle of the bowl. Cover the center with mustard and cress.
- Arrange the radish slices around the salad and spoon over the vinaigrette.

Preparation Time: 10 minutes.
Cooking Time: 10 minutes.

Variation
Chick Pea and Cress Salad
Use a 7-ounce can chick peas tossed in vinaigrette in place of the eggs. A blanched sweet red pepper, deseeded and cut into strips, will add color and flavor to the chick peas.

Warm Red Cabbage with Goat's Cheese

Serves 4

12 ounces red cabbage, shredded
4 tablespoons olive oil, 1 onion, diced
3 tablespoons red wine vinegar
pepper
2 tablespoons chopped chives
6 ounces goat's cheese, crumbled

- Arrange the cabbage in a heatproof bowl.
- Heat the oil in a pan and gently cook the onion over a low heat for about 5 minutes. Add the vinegar to the pan and then pour the mixture onto the cabbage and sprinkle with the cheese and chives. Sprinkle with pepper and mix.

Preparation Time: 10-15 minutes.

Summer Squash & Pepper Slaw

Serves 4

2 summer squashes
3 small red peppers, deseeded
1 onion, thinly sliced
⅔ cup cider vinegar
2 teaspoons salt
1 tablespoon chopped basil
¼ teaspoon dried marjoram
(or 1 teaspoon fresh)
¼ teaspoon dried chili pepper

- Cut the squashes and peppers into matchstick strips. Put into a heatproof bowl with the onion and mix.
- Put the remaining ingredients into a small pan and bring to the boil. Pour over the pepper mixture and leave to stand in the refrigerator for 2 hours.
- Stir before serving

Preparation Time: 15 minutes plus 2 hours standing time.

Spinach & Radicchio Salad

Serves 4

12 ounces fresh spinach, washed
1 head radicchio, washed and dried
4 ounces mushrooms, thinly sliced
3 scallions, thinly sliced
2 hard-boiled eggs, chopped
½ cup goat's cheese, crumbled
1 bunch watercress, washed
For the dressing
6 tablespoons olive oil
3 tablespoons cider vinegar
½ teaspoon sugar
½ teaspoon dried mustard
Salt and pepper
1 clove garlic, cut into 4

- Put the torn spinach, radiccio and mushrooms into a bowl together with the onions and eggs.
- Measure the ingredients for the dressing into a screw-top jar and shake vigorously. Allow to stand for 30 minutes, time permitting.
- Strain the dressing over the salad to remove

the garlic and mix well.
- Add the watercress sprigs and crumbled cheese on top

Preparation Time: 20 minutes.
Cooking Time: 10 minutes for eggs.

Californian Salad

Serves 4
2 small crisp lettuces,
washed and torn into pieces
2 avocados, peeled and pitted
2 tablespoons lemon juice
$^1\!/_2$ cup shelled walnuts, roughly chopped
1 grapefruit, white pith removed
For the dressing
6 tablespoons olive oil
2 tablespoons white wine vinegar
1 tablespoon chopped parsley
1 clove garlic, crushed
$^1\!/_2$ teaspoon salt
$^1\!/_2$ teaspoon dried oregano
Pepper

- Put all the ingredients for the dressing into a screw-top jar and shake to mix. Allow to stand for 15 minutes.
- Arrange the lettuces in a bowl.
- Slice the avocado in strips and put into a dish with lemon juice.
- Sprinkle the walnuts on the lettuce.
- Peel the grapefruit with a sharp knife removing all the white pith. Cut out each segment leaving the skin behind. Arrange on the lettuce.
- Add the avocado, and shaking the dressing well, pour it over the salad.

Preparation Time: 30 minutes including 15 minutes standing time.

Egg and Cress Salad

Mushrooms à la Grecque

Serves 4
Rind and juice of 1 lemon
2 tablespoons olive oil
1 bouquet garni
1 bay leaf
6 peppercorns, slightly crushed
$\frac{1}{2}$ teaspoon coriander seeds, slightly crushed
$\frac{1}{4}$ teaspoon soy sauce
1 stalk of celery, cut into 4 pieces
3 cups button mushrooms, washed
$\frac{1}{4}$ cup dry white wine
Freshly ground black pepper

- Thinly remove the rind from the lemon and cut it into fine strips. Squeeze out the juice. Pour into a pan with 1 cup water and half the oil. Bring to the boil.
- Add the bay leaf, peppercorns, coriander seeds, soy sauce and celery to the pan with the mushrooms and bring to the boil. Simmer for 4 minutes. Add the wine and simmer for another 2 minutes.
- Turn out of the pan into a bowl, sprinkle with pepper. Cover and chill for several hours in the refrigerator.
- Remove the celery, bouquet garni and bay leaf. Drain the mushrooms, retaining the juice. Arrange in a serving dish with a little juice poured over and the remaining oil drizzled over the top. Garnish with some fine strips of lemon rind.

Preparation Time: 10 minutes plus 2 hours chilling time.
Cooking Time: 6 minutes.

Variation
Small pickling onions, artichoke hearts and leeks may all be prepared in this way to be served as a starter or salad.

Onions will need a slightly longer cooking time than mushrooms. Canned artichoke hearts should be gently heated without boiling.

Green Pepper & Raisin Salad

Serves 4
3 sweet green peppers, deseeded
6 scallions, $\frac{1}{3}$ cup raisins
3 tablespoons walnut oil, salt and pepper

- Cut the peppers into strips and plunge into boiling water for 2 minutes. Drain and dry, arrange in a dish and sprinkle over with oil and seasoning.
- Trim the scallions and cut into small slices. Add to the pepper strips. Allow to stand for at least 30 minutes.
- Mix the raisins with the peppers and scallions.

• Line the bottom of a salad dish with the torn lettuce (optional) and tip the pepper mixture on top.

Preparation Time: 15 minutes plus 30 minutes standing time.

Cooking Time: 2 minutes.

Variation

A red onion, finely sliced, can be used in

place of the scallions. 1 tablespoon lemon juice can be added to the oil when marinating the peppers. Three different colored peppers would enliven and add interest to the salad while sliced celery can also be added together with white seedless grapes.

Quick Mixed Bean Salad

Serves 4-6
14-ounce can kidney beans, drained
7-ounce can chick peas, drained
14-ounce can navy beans, drained
4 ounces small fresh green beans
Salt and pepper
$^1/_2$ cup Vinaigrette (page 38)
1 tablespoon chopped parsley
2 scallions, finely chopped
1 red chili pepper, deseeded and finely chopped (optional)
$^1/_2$ sweet red pepper,
deseeded and cut into small dice

• Tip the drained beans into a salad bowl and mix well.
• Cook the French beans for 4 minutes in a little boiling salted water. Drain and run under cold water to cool. Dry on kitchen paper and add to the canned beans. Season the beans with salt and pepper.
• Pour the vinaigrette onto the beans and sprinkle with chopped parsley. Stand in the refrigerator for 30 minutes.
• Prepare the scallions, chili and red pepper and mix well. Sprinkle on the beans just before serving.

Preparation Time: 20 minutes plus 30 minutes standing time.

Cooking Time: 4 minutes.

Variation

Mixed Bean Salad with Cottage and Blue Cheeses

Make up the bean salad as above (the chili and sweet red pepper can be omitted). Top with 1 cup cottage cheese mixed with $^1/_4$ cup crumbled blue cheese. Serve as a topping to the bean salad.

Warm Potato Salad

Serves 4
8 ounces new potatoes, halved
8 ounces sweet potato,
cut into cubes
3 tablespoons olive oil
1 tablespoon lemon juice
2 stalks celery, sliced
4 scallions, finely chopped
$^1/_2$ small red cabbage, finely shredded
For the dressing
8 tablespoons olive oil
3 tablespoons white wine vinegar
Salt and pepper
1 tablespoon parsley
1 tablespoon dill
1 tablespoon French mustard

• Cook the new potatoes in boiling salted water for 10 minutes, adding the cubes of sweet potato for the last 5 minutes. Drain well and dry on kitchen paper.
• Heat the oil in a large pan and add both batches of potatoes and fry until golden, then add 4 tablespoons water and the lemon juice. Cover and cook for about 10 minutes until the potatoes are tender.
• Stir the celery and scallions into the potatoes. Arrange the shredded cabbage in a heated serving dish.
• Mix the dressing in a screw-top jar and shake well. Tip over the potatoes and then spoon back into the salad bowl with the red cabbage. Serve at once.

Preparation Time: 20 minutes.

Cooking Time: 20-25 minutes.

OPPOSITE: *Green Pepper & Raisin Salad*

Beet, Orange & Apple Mold

Serves 4
1 pound cooked beets,
skinned and sliced
1 apple peeled, cored and sliced
2 oranges, cut into segments
2 cups Beetroot Stock (page 14)
2 teaspoons agar

• Cut the beet slices into halves about the same size as the apple slices. Prepare the orange by peeling off the skin and white pith and cutting into segments with a sharp knife, leaving all the skin behind.
• Heat half the beetroot stock to boiling and dissolve the agar. Add the remaining cooled stock. Rinse a large mold with cold water. Arrange some beets, orange and apple slices on the bottom and pour in some liquid stock and agar. Place in the refrigerator and allow to set.
• Remove and set another layer of stock with apples and beetroot arranged in it. Continue until all the ingredients except a few segments of orange are used.
• Allow the whole mold to set and then turn out and serve with a green salad garnished with beets and oranges.

Preparation Time: 2-3 hours including setting time.

Orange & Celery Salad

Serves 4
12 lettuce leaves, washed and dried
2 oranges,
skinned and cut into segments
8 stalks celery,
strings removed and thinly sliced
4 scallions, white parts only,
finely sliced
Vinaigrette (page 38)

• Tear the lettuce leaves and line a salad bowl.
• Mix the oranges and celery with the scallions and toss in the dressing. Tip into the salad bowl.

Preparation Time: 10 minutes.

Old-Fashioned Potato Salad

Serves 4-6
1½ pounds cooked new potatoes, diced
1¼ cups Mayonnaise (page 35)
Salt and freshly ground pepper
1 tablespoon white wine vinegar
2 teaspoons French mustard
½ teaspoon celery seeds
4 stalks celery, thinly sliced
4 scallions, thinly sliced
4 hard-boiled eggs
For the garnish
6 radishes, thinly sliced
2 tablespoons parsley

• Place the diced potatoes in a salad bowl with the mayonnaise, seasoning, vinegar, mustard, celery seeds, celery, and scallions. Gently fold the ingredients together making sure not to break up the potatoes.
• Remove the egg yolks, set aside. Chop the egg whites, add to the potatoes.
• Arrange the radishes around the dish. Sprinkle the salad with chopped parsley. Sieve the egg yolk on top.

Preparation Time: 15 minutes.
Cooking Time: 30 minutes.

Beet Salad

Serves 4
1 pound uncooked beets, coarsely grated
2 dessert apples, thinly sliced
1 onion, peeled and finely sliced
For the dressing
2 tablespoons lemon juice
salt and pepper
1 cup Mayonnaise (page 35)
2 tablespoons grated horseradish

• Mix beets, apples and onions together in a bowl.
• Combine all the ingredients for the dressing, mixing well, then mix into the salad.

Preparation Time: 15 minutes.

Variation
Serve with wedges of hard-boiled egg.

Bean Salad with Pineapple

Serves 4
8 ounces lima beans,
soaked overnight
2 carrots, sliced lengthways into sticks
14-ounce can pineapple, drained
1 cup bean sprouts
1 tablespoon lemon juice
Salt and pepper
2 teaspoons chopped fresh marjoram

• Drain the beans and cook in boiling water for about 45 minutes until tender. (Use drained canned beans if time is short.) Drain and allow to cool.
• Cook the carrots in boiling salted water until tender but still firm. Drain and cool. Mix the carrots with the lima beans in a salad bowl.
• Cut the pineapple into small squares and add to the beans. Mix well and add the bean sprouts. Pour over the lemon juice, sprinkle with salt, pepper and marjoram.
• Add a few drops of pineapple juice and mix well before serving.
   Serve a Vinaigrette (page 38) or yogurt and lemon dressing separately.

Preparation: 10 minutes plus 8 hours soaking time.
Cooking Time: 45 minutes.

OPPOSITE: *Beet, Orange & Apple Mold*

Strawberry & Avocado Salad

Serves 4

1 pound strawberries, stalks removed
Freshly ground black pepper
8 ounces young spinach leaves, washed and dried
2 ripe avocados, peeled
2 tablespoons lemon juice
4 tablespoons light cream
Salt and pepper
$1/4$ cup pine nuts

• Arrange a few spinach leaves on each plate. Cut the strawberries in half, reserving a few, and arrange on top of the spinach leaves sprinkling with freshly ground black pepper.
• Cut the avocados in half, then cut each half into 6 slices and sprinkle with lemon juice to prevent discoloration. Arrange with the strawberries and spinach leaves.
• Mix the cream with salt and pepper and spread over the fruit and vegetables. Arrange the remaining strawberries in the center of each plate and sprinkle with the pine nuts.

Preparation Time: 15 minutes.

BELOW: Strawberry & Avocado Salad
OPPOSITE: Rice & Lychee Salad

Chili Eggs Vinaigrette

Serves 4

8 hard-boiled eggs
3 celery stalks, sliced
4 scallions, finely chopped
12 pimento-stuffed olives, sliced
3 tablespoons olive oil
2 tablespoons red wine vinegar
$1/2$ teaspoon chili paste

• Place the eggs in a serving dish, yolk sides up. Sprinkle with the celery, scallions and olives.
• Put the oil, vinegar and chili paste in a screw-top jar. Shake well and pour over the eggs. Serve immediately with warm French or wholewheat bread.

Preparation Time: 10 minutes.
Cooking Time: 15 minutes.

Rice & Lychee Salad

Serves 4

2 cups cooked brown or white long-grain rice

²/₃ cup Vinaigrette (page 38)

1 onion, finely chopped

1 red and 1 yellow pepper, halved and deseeded

1 cup shredded white cabbage

8 fresh lychees, peeled and pitted

For the garnish

1 tablespoon chopped parsley

Lemon wedges

• Mix the rice with the vinaigrette in a bowl. Add the onion, mix thoroughly, and allow to stand for 10 minutes.

• Blanch the peppers for 4 minutes in boiling salted water. Drain and cool under cold water and cut into thin strips.

• Arrange the rice mixture in a suitable dish, arranging the pepper strips and lychees on top. Sprinkle with the parsley and serve with wedges of lemon.

Preparation Time: 20 minutes.
Cooking Time: 25 minutes.

Desserts

Fresh fruit should be an integral part of a healthy diet, packed full as it is with minerals and vitamins as well as being a source of useful fiber. A piece of fresh fruit is a better choice to round off a meal than an elaborate pudding, however delicious, which is often packed with fat and sugar. Many people, especially children, though loath to eat a piece of fresh fruit will happily tuck into a pudding. It is medically recommended that five servings of fruit and vegetables are consumed daily and serving a fruity dessert is one way of making sure everyone comes near to fulfilling this quota. Chop up fresh fruit and serve it with yogurt and ice cream. Cook fruit lightly, and only where necessary, with the minimum of added sugar and save those favorite, calorie-laden desserts for special occasions!

Summer Pudding

This delicious pudding can also be made in winter with frozen berries.

Serves 4-6
*2 pounds mixed berries
(raspberries, strawberries, blueberries, red or
black currants, blackberries, loganberries
and cherries (pitted), $^3/_4$ cup sugar
1 white sandwich loaf, medium-sliced*

- Pick over the fruit and remove the stalks. Rinse very gently in a colander and place in a pan with the sugar and 3 tablespoons water. Bring slowly to the boil and simmer gently until the fruit has softened while still retaining its shape. Allow to cool and taste for sweetness. Add a little more sugar if necessary but do not make the mixture too sweet or the flavor will be spoiled.
- Remove the crusts from the bread and cut each slice in half. Stand a $1^1/_2$-pint pudding basin on a plate.
- Strain the juice from the fruit into a jug. Line the bottom of the bowl with the bread, cutting it to fit, then line the sides with the bread fingers so that they are a snug fit with no gaps in between.
- Spoon some of the juice over the bread lining the base and sides. Half fill the bowl with fruit, put a layer of bread on top and fill the top half with the remainder of the fruit. Finish with more fingers of bread.
- Pour the remaining juice over the top and around the sides, reserving at least 1 tablespoon. Fit a round plate over the top of the bowl and stand a heavy can or weight on top. Allow to stand overnight or for several hours.
- To unmold the pudding, place a serving dish (one with enough space to hold the juice) on top of the bowl and invert. If there are any small white patches of bread still showing, spoon over the extra juice.
- Decorate with fresh fruit and mint leaves. Serve with a raspberry or strawberry purée and cream.

  An alternative, though messier, method is to dip each piece of bread into the juice before lining the bowl.

Preparation Time: 20 minutes (35 if using fresh fruit) plus standing time.
Cooking Time: 10 minutes.

Summer Pudding

Summer Fruit Salad

Summer Fruit Salad

Choose any favorite fruits in season.
Serves 4
2 peaches or nectarines, peeled and pitted
8 ounces strawberries
8 ounces raspberries
4 ounces each cherries and plums, pitted
For the cream
³/₄ cup light cream
2 tablespoons caster sugar
1 teaspoon grated orange peel
1 tablespoon fresh orange juice

• Slice the peaches or nectarines and place in a large bowl or in individual serving dishes. Gently wash the strawberries and raspberries, removing the stalks; pat dry with kitchen paper and add to the dishes. Arrange the cherries and plums on top and chill for at least 30 minutes.

• Mix the cream with the sugar, orange peel and juice. Chill also before serving with the fruit salad.

Preparation Time: 15 minutes plus chilling time.
Use limes instead of oranges, if preferred.

119

Poached Pears

Serves 4
*4 ripe dessert pears,
peeled but with stalks left intact*
$\frac{1}{2}$ cup sugar
*$\frac{1}{2}$ teaspoon vanilla essence or
1 tablespoon Poire Williams liqueur
or kirsch*

- Put the sugar in a deep pan with $\frac{1}{2}$ cup water and the sugar. Allow to dissolve and add the pears and the flavorings.
- Poach gently for about 15 minutes until the pears are just tender. Leave to cool in the syrup.
- Carefully lift each pear onto a dessert plate. Spoon over the syrup and decorate with mint leaves.

Preparation Time: 10 minutes plus cooling time.
Cooking Time: 15 minutes.

Variations

Pears in White Wine

Cook the pears in the syrup as in previous recipe. Transfer the pears to a serving dish. Add $\frac{1}{2}$ cup white wine to the syrup and simmer gently for 10 minutes. Pour the syrup over the pears and allow to cool before serving.

Pears Belle-Hélène

Cook the pears as for Poached Pears and allow to cool in the syrup. Make a rich chocolate sauce by melting 4 ounces dark chocolate very gently in a small pan with 3 tablespoons water. When dissolved, add 1 tablespoon of rum. Keep warm in a jug standing in warm water. Serve poured over the drained cold pears. Vanilla or rum ice cream can be served on the side.

New England Baked Apples

Serves 4
4 medium to large cooking apples, washed
For the filling
2 tablespoons butter or margarine
$\frac{1}{2}$ cup currants, $\frac{1}{4}$ cup walnuts, chopped
1 teaspoon cinnamon
For the sauce
4 tablespoons unsweetened apple juice
1 tablespoon maple syrup
1 tablespoon brown sugar

- Preheat the oven to 400°F.
- Core the apples, making sure not to go right through their bases and put them in an ovenproof dish.
- Mix all the filling ingredients together in a small bowl. Stuff the filling carefully into the center hollows of the apples.
- Mix the apple juice and syrup together and pour around the apples. Sprinkle with sugar and bake in the oven for 45 minutes. Serve hot or cold with the remaining syrup, cream, custard or ice cream.

Preparation Time: 15 minutes.
Cooking Time: 45 minutes.

ABOVE: *Poached Pears*

OPPOSITE: *New England Baked Apples*

Orange Bread & Butter Pudding

Serves 4

12 slices of white or brown bread, buttered

$^1/_2$ cup sultanas (optional)

$1^1/_4$ cups milk

$^1/_2$ cup light cream

2 eggs, beaten

$^1/_4$ cup superfine sugar

Grated zest of 1 orange

- Preheat the oven to 375°F. Butter a shallow ovenproof baking dish.
- Cut the bread into squares and arrange in the dish. Sprinkle the sultanas between the slices, if using.
- Mix the milk, cream, eggs, sugar and orange zest together in a jug or bowl. Pour over the bread and, if time allows, stand to allow the bread to absorb the mixture for up to 1 hour.
- Bake in the oven for 45 minutes until the mixture is set and the top is golden brown. Serve with cream or custard.

Preparation Time: 20 minutes.
Cooking Time: 45 minutes.

This is an excellent way of using up slightly stale bread.

Spiced Fruit Pie

Serves 4-6

8 ounces Rich Pie Pastry (pages 94-95)

$^1/_4$ cup soft brown sugar

2 tablespoons white sugar

1 tablespoon all-purpose flour

$^1/_4$ teaspoon grated nutmeg

$^1/_4$ teaspoon ground cinnamon

Finely grated rind of 1 orange

Finely grated rind of $^1/_2$ lemon

1 tablespoon lemon juice

$2^1/_4$ pounds pears, apples, peaches, cherries or plums

$^1/_4$ cup sultanas (optional)

To finish

1 tablespoon milk

1 tablespoon caster sugar

- Lightly grease a deep 8-inch pie dish. Make the pastry and allow to rest. At the end of the resting period, preheat the oven to 400°F.
- Roll out half the pastry and line the bottom of the pie dish. Cut off a strip, damp the lip of the pie dish and line with the pastry strip.
- Peel, core or stone the selection of fruit and then cut into even sized slices. Mix the brown and white sugars, the flour and spices. Sprinkle some on the bottom of the pastry and follow this with a layer of fruit. Sprinkle this layer with some rind, juice and sultanas.
- Continue layering sugar, fruit and other ingredients until all are used up.
- Roll out the remaining piece of pastry into a round or oval to suit the dish. Make it 2 inches larger than the dish. Dampen the edges of the rim.
- Lift the pastry onto the fruit, press gently together without stretching and then press the rims together. Trim the edge with a knife.
- Brush with milk and sprinkle with sugar. Bake in the oven for 20 minutes and then turn the oven down to 375°F and continue cooking for a further 20 minutes. Serve with custard or cream.

Preparation Time: 30 minutes plus resting time for pastry.
Cooking Time: 40 minutes.

Crêpes Suzette

Serves 4

$^1/_2$ cup unsalted butter

Finely grated peel of 1 orange

Juice of 1-2 oranges

$^1/_2$ cup caster sugar

8 thin Crêpes (page 63)

2 tablespoons Grand Marnier or Orange Curaçao

2 tablespoons brandy

- Cream the butter in a bowl with the peel, a little juice and the caster sugar. Add as much juice as the mixture will take without curdling. Only use 2 oranges if they are not very juicy. This butter can be made in advance and kept in the refrigerator. The

pancakes can also be made in advance.

- Heat the prepared butter in a frying pan and add the crêpes to the melted mixture one at a time, spooning the mixture over. Fold in half, then in four, and push to one side. Continue until all the crêpes have been folded, then pour in the liqueur. Warm the brandy on a ladle and set it alight. Pour onto the crêpes and serve immediately with the sauce.

Preparation Time: 15 minutes plus 30 minutes standing time for crêpes.
Cooking Time: 20 minutes.

Winter Fruit Compote

Serves 4

3 dessert apples, peeled and sliced

3 pears, peeled and sliced

3 peaches, peeled and sliced

4 apricots, sliced

$^1/_4$ cup raisins or sultanas

$^1/_4$ cup pistachios, shelled

For the syrup

$2^1/_2$ cups water

$^3/_4$ cup sugar

Juice of 1 lemon

- Put all the prepared fruits and raisins or sultanas into a large saucepan together with the ingredients for the syrup.
- Bring to the boil, then simmer gently for about 15 minutes or so until the fruits begin to disintegrate and the raisins have plumped up.
- Allow to cool, mix with the pistachios and transfer to individual serving dishes.

Preparation Time: 10 minutes plus soaking time.
Cooking Time: 30 minutes.

Almost any combination of fruits can be used for this dish, including dried fruits which would need to be soaked before cooking. Retain the soaking liquor and use it to provide extra flavor when cooking the fruit.

RIGHT: Winter Fruit Compote

Fruit Kebabs

Serves 4
$^1/_2$ cup grapes, seeds removed
*1 thick slice of watermelon, peeled
and cubed*
*2 firm but ripe nectarines, peeled and
cut into segments*
2 small juicy oranges, peeled and segmented
A little brown sugar
2 tablespoons warmed brandy
$^1/_2$ cup thick Greek-style yogurt

- Prepare the fruits and cut or segment into even-sized pieces. Lightly oil four skewers or kebab sticks and arrange the different fruits alternately on these.
- Sprinkle the fruits with sugar and broil under a fierce heat for 1-2 minutes each side or on a barbecue, turning once. Spoon a little warmed brandy over the kebabs before serving, or spoon over and, holding carefully with thick gloves, return to the barbecue to flame quickly before serving with a little yogurt.

Tip
When barbecuing kebabs it is best to use long sticks or skewers, filled only one third to half full to make them easier to handle.

Preparation Time: 15 minutes.
Cooking Time: 1-2 minutes.

Fruit Sundae

Serves 2
Blueberry sorbet or ice cream
2 tablespoons blueberry jelly
$^1/_2$ cup blueberries or blackcurrants
$^1/_2$ cup strawberries, destalked and halved
1 ripe peach, peeled and cut into segments
For the garnish
A few sprigs of mint

- Allow the sorbet or ice cream to soften slightly for a few minutes to make it easier handle.
- Warm the jelly slightly, covered, in a microwave oven and add to the blueberries or blackcurrants, mixing well. Spoon half into the bases of two tall sundae glasses.
- Top with one scoop of sorbet or ice cream

and a selection of fruit. Add more sorbet or ice cream and serve with sprigs of mint.

Preparation Time: 15 minutes.

ABOVE: *Fruit Sundae*
OPPOSITE: *Fruit Kebabs*

Caramelized Oranges

Serves 4

1/2 cup granulated sugar
4 large oranges
5 tablespoons water

- Place the sugar in a heavy-based pan with 3 tablespoons water. Allow to dissolve over a low heat then boil gently without stirring until the syrup turns golden.
- Remove thin strips of peel from the orange, avoiding the bitter white pith. Place in a small bowl with 2 tablespoons boiling water. Carefully remove all remaining pith from the oranges, retaining any juice, and place whole into a serving dish.
- Once the syrup has turned golden, plunge the pan into a sink of cold water to arrest the process and prevent burning. Quickly add the peel, water and juice to the syrup which will bubble furiously. Stir gently until blended, then pour over the oranges. Chill until ready to serve.

Preparation Time: 30 minutes.
Cooking Time: 15 minutes.

ABOVE: *Caramelized Oranges*
RIGHT: *Citrus Salad Jelly*

Citrus Fruit Jelly

Serves 4

2 large oranges
2 large grapefruit
3/4 cup sugar
3/4 cup fresh orange juice
1 teaspoon agar
For the garnish
Sprigs of mint or fruit

- Carefully remove half the peel from an orange and a grapefruit and cut it into fine matchsticks. Place in a small bowl of warm water to soften. Remove all the peel and white pith from the rest of the fruits.
- Remove the flesh from the fruits, cutting carefully between the segments to leave unwanted fibers and strings behind and catching excess juices in a small bowl. Add to the orange juice and make up to 1^1/$_2$ cups with water. Sprinkle the fruit slices with sugar and set aside.
- Dissolve the agar in the liquid, bring to the boil and cook for one minute. Allow to cool slightly, stirring frequently, then quickly layer the fruit with the jelly in a 1-lb loaf tin or mold, keeping the different fruits separate. The jelly will begin to set very quickly but will need a further thorough chilling for 1-2 hours before serving
- Quickly tip the peel matchsticks out onto a sheet of paper or foil and sprinkle them lightly with more sugar. Add 3 tablespoons water to a heavy or non-stick pan with ^{1}/$_2$ cup of sugar. Dissolve over a low heat until dissolved, then boil gently until the syrup slightly caramelizes.
- To serve, cut the jelly into slices and decorate each portion with a few shreds of sugared zest, some caramel sauce, sprigs of mint and small fruits.

Preparation Time: 30 minutes.
Cooking Time: 15 minutes.

Index

Page numbers in *italics* refer to illustrations